EVERYDAY IMPACT

Erinfeng

to: Selina Zeng

Thank you for many years of friendship Selina!
You are a continued inspiration, and I wish you
amazing success in your future!

EVERYDAY IMPACT

EMBARK ON A JOURNEY OF IMPACT:
THE 3 I'S OF MEANINGFUL CHANGE

ERIN FENG

NEW DEGREE PRESS

EVERYDAY IMPACT
Embark on a Journey of Impact: The 3 I's of Meaningful Change

ISBN   978-1-63676-940-0 *Paperback*
           978-1-63730-006-0 *Kindle Ebook*
           978-1-63730-108-1 *Ebook*

To My Loving Feng Family,
With utmost love and gratitude for everything
you have helped me to do.

To my friends and mentors,
This journey of impact would not have been possible without you.

TABLE OF CONTENTS

———

Be the change you wish to see in the world.

—MAHATMA GANDHI

INTRODUCTION: EMBARKING ON YOUR JOURNEY OF IMPACT

—

The concept of the "golden ticket is a beautiful notion made ubiquitous by the timeless tale of *Charlie and the Chocolate Factory*. But while the story of a poor yet deserving child's life being changed by a single, magical event is moving, the idea can seem to be more rooted in fiction than reality.[1]

In one case, however, a principal's act of kindness and a $10 ticket was what led magician Claude Haggerty down a path of magic and giving. What he did afterward truly shows how the coveted "golden ticket" might not be so fictional after all.

As a stuttering foster kid, Claude was a target for bullying and constantly put down. But one fateful day, after telling his

---

1   Roald Dahl, *Charlie and the Chocolate Factory* (New York: Alfred A. Knopf Inc, 1964), 1-176.

principal about his magician dreams, Claude's life changed forever. His principal supported him to pursue his magical aspirations, going as far as to buy a $10 ticket to take him to a big magic show in their city.

Years later, Claude became an innovative magician dedicated to impact and service. He paid forward the kindness from his teachers by partnering with schools to deliver engaging magic shows that empowered elementary students to pursue their own dreams. Over his career, he raised millions for nonprofits and brought community organizations together to create partnerships and augment their impact.

Claude's story is inspiring, but it definitely doesn't fit the normal thoughts we have about creating impact; to make a ton of money and then setting up a nonprofit. He simply was doing what he loved—and having his passion drive impact.

I found it interesting to note how his principal's small act of kindness turned out to have such massive impact, seeming to compound over time to help foster a changemaker within Claude. Intrigued, I wanted to understand if Claude's story was unique or part of a much larger trend.

What I discovered has changed the entire way I see how all of us can drive impact every day to make the world a better place.

***

Our world is filled with stories of impact. The inspirational narratives of going from the bottom to the top can be found within anyone, but what seems to dominate headlines are the stories of big names and big money.

"Tesla Energy's role in the fight for a sustainable future explained by Elon Musk."[2]

"Jeff Bezos commits $10 billion to fight climate change."[3]

These headlines show a single-minded focus on world-renowned corporations, famous CEOs, and philanthropic checks beyond our wildest dreams. While admirable, the monopolized media dissemination of these gargantuan contributions can be counter-intuitive. Think about how we feel when we consider the vastness of the world, as the realization that we're just a speck in the seven billion people on this earth brings about waves of insecurity. In the same way, these contributions can make our impact seem like pennies.

Indeed, there is a danger in considering the monumental things as it can lead to a sobering realization of one's own insignificance and incompetence. We want to surrender to the higher power and yield our responsibilities. In this way, next to these renowned figures and organizations, we can lose sight of the unique potential in ourselves. Any contribution can seem meaningless in comparison to the accomplishments of established figures like Bezos.

After all, why bother when others are already doing the work?

---

2   Simon Alvarez, "Tesla Energy's role in the fight for a sustainable future explained by Elon Musk," *Teslarati*, July 23, 2020.

3   Tom Metcalf, "Jeff Bezos Donating US$10B Barely Dents his Surging Fortune," *Bloomberg News*, Feb. 18, 2020.

But I didn't feel satisfied with this answer. Rather, I couldn't accept it. Was this all there is? Should we leave the impactful actions to the nonprofits and CEOs?

Is a big, philanthropic cash check the only impact that will make a difference?

***

I am on a journey. I know what I want, but I don't know how I can get there.

Growing up in a family of immigrants, I learned the importance of support and sacrifice at a young age. With an innate sense of altruism and a passion for serving others, I knew that I wanted to do something in the future where I could make a positive difference in the lives of people around me. But I was never certain about how I wanted to pursue this impact.

Being raised by traditional Chinese parents meant that there were only three paths of life: medicine, law, and business. The fundamental goal was what my parents considered to be the great "North American life": to raise a family, own a big house, go on vacation a few times a year, and retire at the ripe old age of sixty. As a kid, this self-centered lifestyle was the only one I was taught.

I was fortunate that one of those three paths of life turned out to become an interest of mine. Business fascinated me in the power and influence that organizations hold. I was enamored by the image of the corporate lifestyle, enraptured by the mantra that "business makes the world go-'round."[4] However, business never had the best reputation; it was considered the "dog-eat-dog world," where profit was everything and people would do anything to get it.[5]

This image never sat right with me, and my altruistic self couldn't accept that my success could only be the product of a zero-sum outcome.

This all changed when I learned about Corporate Social Responsibility (CSR) in grade ten. I learned how business could be used to better the lives of stakeholders—every person that could potentially be impacted by the business—and began to appreciate the potential of business in creating a positive community and societal impact. This idea was then reinforced in grade eleven when I participated in the Foundation for Student Science and Technology Online Research Coop.[6] In it, I worked as the research assistant for an NGO advocating against child sex trafficking and helped them calculate the economic benefits of preventing one child from falling victim to trafficking.

This life-changing experience allowed me to experience firsthand just how business concepts and organizations could create a positive difference in our world and change lives. From there, something clicked into place like a stray puzzle piece; I found motivation in creating a positive impact on

---

4   Kristin Zhivago, "Business Makes the World Go Round," *Kristin's Wisdom* (blog), Sept. 10, 2018.

5   "Dog Eat Dog," Investopedia, accessed December 20, 2020.

6   "Online Research Coop Program," The Journal of Student Science and Technology, accessed December 18, 2020.

others. Since then, I have been driven by the desire to create lasting change in my future communities.

Now at this point, I'd identified my goal, but I didn't know the exact path I wanted to take to get there. I'd set the location in the GPS of my life, but I couldn't choose between the innumerable routes to travel.

When we think about creating an impact, we think about needing to be influential and wealthy like a CEO and creating our own nonprofit. I was originally no exception to this understanding. During the CSR unit in grade ten, our examples only featured major companies, including Tim Hortons and Walmart. I would only hear news about what major philanthropist CEOs and nonprofits were doing to impact the world, which perpetuated this mutually exclusive outlook of impact being reserved for the charitable and nonprofit sector.

I remember feeling disillusioned, questioning whether I could make it in the social impact community if big names and big money were required to make positive change. Nonetheless, I was determined not to give up on my heart to serve and set out on a journey of impact to meet others who were changing the communities around them for the better in a desperate attempt for inspiration and guidance. What I found changed the way I thought about impact forever.

***

Too often people constrain the idea of creating impact into one industry: nonprofits. However, this view is misguided and untrue. The turn of the new decade with 2020 brought to light many new and existing challenges in our society. From systematic racism to a need for acts of kindness, change is necessary in order to achieve and maintain sustainable, positive progress. And importantly, people must know that they can create an impact no matter where or who they are.

Social impact, to me, is defined by any action that creates a change in the people and communities around you.

With the influence of media and perception of the social impact field, the contributions of CEOs and massive non-profits are always on the front pages. Yet this trend can be isolating, as it perpetuates the idea that a difference can only be created if you're this big figure with the financial means and professional connections to do so.

When we focus on such events, rather than their intended inspirational use, it can breed the thought: "That's insane, I could never reach such a level." We've heard in the past that hearing about global issues makes it difficult to believe that just one person can make a difference. But when the spotlight is focused on the contributions of major corporations and philanthropists, we start to believe that our small contributions will seem null next to the billions of philanthropic investments. So why even bother?

It ultimately perpetuates the thought that impact has to be big to be considered meaningful and disseminates the counterproductive "go-big-or-go-home" mentality.

But I believe something else.

Through my interviews and research, I've come to understand a better, more sustainable way of looking at impact. Governments and nonprofits are not the only forces that can change and impact lives.

According to Ann Mei Chang, an experienced chief innovation officer and author of *Lean Impact*, "Aid and charity only represent about 2 percent of spending in developing countries. Private investment is blossoming."[7] These statistics show that impact and giving have shifted away from being constrained to the nonprofit sector. Presenting more potential in the private sector, we see that individuals and private corporations can create meaningful impact, not just nonprofits.

I believe that anyone can make an impact on their everyday lives, and small, regular acts can compound over time to drive long-term change. And Claude's story serves as real proof that even small actions can make a massive difference.

Claude was no CEO of a big company, nor was he entirely dedicated to the nonprofit industry; he used his passion as a way to drive impactful actions. By paying the kindness that his principal showed to him forward to other students, Claude shows how small acts of kindness, some kind words and a simple $10 ticket, can change someone's life and allow that person to impact others. Essentially, that small act has compounded over time into something much greater—a gift

---

7   *TEDx Talks,* "Ending Global Poverty: Let's Think Like Silicon Valley | Ann Mei Chang | TEDxMidAtlantic," Jan. 10, 2017, Video, 12:24.

that keeps on giving. This incredible compounding process is what I call "Everyday Impact."

Having put this concept to name, I was motivated by a desire to share this philosophy with others through a book that explicitly addresses this idea.

Currently, many resources on achieving positive social impact often are not able to make that connection to their audience. They may resonate with the truly ambitious individuals, but others who may not resonate with such an ambitious demographic may feel disconnected. When such resources limit themselves to covering only the massive impact initiatives and focus on the scale of the impact created from the get-go, many readers may lose hope and feel disheartened.

This book seeks to address that gap. I hope to remind any individual, disheartened or otherwise, that positive impact is important and valuable no matter how big or small. Importantly, we must be reminded that even the smallest actions can lead to big differences. I felt compelled to write this book in order to show that anyone can make an impact regardless of their wealth, fame, or industry.

As I explored the community of changemakers that I'd developed and researched, I came to meet and learn the stories of some truly amazing people, but none of whom were exactly the way I expected them to be.

Many of them, like Claude, weren't focused on business and were simply doing what they loved—yet having it drive their impact. Even though they engaged in smaller actions, they made a world of difference.

THE THEORY OF EVERYDAY IMPACT

This book seeks to explain my concept of "Everyday Impact," to promote an understanding of the power of simple acts done now that drive real change and affect those around you, but compound over time to create a greater impact in the future.

My research and interviews have allowed me to see fundamental patterns in stories of impact. They have shown me the stories and contributions of changemakers follow three common principles that help drive meaningful, lasting positive change in their lives unto the lives of others. Under these three principles are similar themes and mantras that support the principle: what I call the "3 I's of Meaningful Change."

Like the mystical concept of the third eye, these 3 I's can also provide a perception beyond ordinary sight, a perspective that transcends that of which is disseminated by the media.[8] It is my hope that these 3 I's can help you to understand the connections and answer your concerns and questions to ultimately lead you to create your own vision.

1. **Inspiration:** Fittingly inspired itself by Simon Sinek's philosophy of "start with why," this first principle

---

8   *Dictionary.com*, s.v. "Third Eye," accessed August 23, 2020.

explores the motivation behind the actions and goals of changemakers.[9]

2. **Impact:** In the second principle, we learn of the actual change that these people have had on others—their success stories, if you will. You'll hear about their methods and processes to gain inspiration about how to create your own change. Notably, placing emphasis on smaller, easy-to-implement actions, the stories of real community changemakers prove that small actions can really make a difference.

3. **Innovation:** The third principle touches on a lesser covered but important aspect for long-lasting, sustainable change. After identifying your inspiration and impact, this section stimulates your mind by providing ideas of how you can go above-and-beyond in your actions to drive unique, positive impact. You'll learn what separates the good from the great and how anyone can go outside of the status quo of their job to create meaningful change.

Trying to find your purpose and path may seem daunting, but you are not alone. Not only is this book filled with stories of people who have been in your very shoes; it also stands as the culmination of my own journey of discovery. So come along with me for the ride, and I hope that you'll be able to come out at the end inspired and filled with ideas to make your own impact in your everyday lives.

---

9   Simon Sinek, *Start with Why: How Great Leaders Inspire Everyone to Take Action* (New York: Portfolio, 2009.) 1-258

WHO IS THIS FOR?

In tandem with this book's goal to show how anyone can make a difference in their everyday lives, this concept of "Everyday Impact" is universal in its application and relevance to all people.

Specific demographics, however, may find stories that they may resonate with more:

1. Young students may find inspiration in the stories of young changemakers and established professionals alike to help guide them achieve a positive impact themselves in the future.

2. Others may be people who are early in their career but feeling unfulfilled. This book can inspire you to use purpose and impact as a way to build the foundation for a prosperous career journey.

3. Still others are the people who are already mid-career, going about the daily responsibilities of their job but burdened by an exigent sense of non-fulfilment. This book can oil your gears of creativity to find a new reason to wake up excited for the day and do good in the world.

Regardless of whether you fit into any of these three described categories, the book was written to inspire anyone to succeed and do more with themselves than just the status quo. It will help you to aspire to go above-and-beyond no matter where you are and find your purpose in giving.

WHAT'S IN IT FOR ME?

This book is designed to inspire and bring a new perspective on what we have conventionally thought to be the notion of social impact. It will change the way you see how all of us can drive impact to make the world a better place by:

- Challenging traditional economic theory by exploring the philosophy of purpose over profit;

- Placing emphasis on a different perspective of renowned purpose-driven brands and people—not simply regurgitating their contributions that you've already heard many times, but rather bringing light to their humble beginnings and how they compounded their impact over time;

- Explaining the ripple effect of impact and how in changing one person's life, you leave your legacy unto every person that individual subsequently influences.

You'll learn the stories of famous changemakers like the founding father of Microfinance, Muhammad Yunus, yet explained in a narrative that is focused on their journeys of growth rather than the size of their impact. The interesting concept of "purpose over profit" will also be explored through the story of Scott Harrison, founder of Charity: Water, and his story of purpose and redemption.

Beyond these conventional stories of more well-known individuals, you will also learn the stories of everyday people who are making a difference in their community using everyday actions. You will read about how they have helped to influence the people around them through small, consistent actions, and how those actions ultimately helped to lead to even greater outcomes. You will learn how even the most average person can leave a lasting impact and legacy. Rather than focusing solely on changing the world, you'll learn how you can implement personal life changes that allow you to drive your very own world of difference.

***

Now is a revolutionary time of impact. Yet we must not get disheartened and be swept up by the "go big or go home" mentality. We must throw the stone of change into the pond of giving to create the ripple effect of positive impact that we want to see. This book is less a solution and more a series of insights and inspirations that will help you reach your own means to an end.

As you begin your journey of impact, I leave you with a shortened quote but one of the most well known in the world from Mahatma Gandhi. Fittingly, this serves as the perfect epitome of my book.

"Be the change you wish to see in the world."[10]

---

10   "Be the Change," Genesis, accessed December 14, 2020.

PART I

HOW WE GOT HERE

CHAPTER 1

A BRIEF HISTORY OF SOCIAL IMPACT

WELCOME TO THE IMPACT REVOLUTION

"Business makes the world go 'round."[11] This is the common adage which we associate with the influence of corporations in our current society. But what is perhaps most interesting is how the role of business has changed in the past few decades.

In 1970 when Milton Friedman published his famous essay "The Social Responsibility of Business Is to Increase Its Profits," the theory that business only had obligations to its shareholders was pushed into the spotlight. A self-interested, profit-maximizing attitude was accepted as business' primary function.[12]

---

11   Kristin Zhivago, "Business Makes the World Go Round," *Kristin's Wisdom* (blog), Sept. 10, 2018.

12   Milton Friedman, "A Friedman Doctrine—The Social Responsibility of Business Is to Increase Its Profits," *The New York Times,* Sept. 13, 1970.

However, the past few decades have seen a shift in this perspective as arguments for their social responsibility beyond profits emerged. Indeed, businesses are now expected to contribute beyond legal requirements to the community and society in which they operate.

This has given rise to the concept of Corporate Social Responsibility (CSR) which encompasses the transformed relationship between state, market, and civil society.[13] The widespread acceptance and adoption of this concept indicate the developing social role of private actors in future governance and society.

Yet this would not have been possible without many of the renowned actors we know today who defined the social impact industry and paved the path for social purpose in business. While this book will tell the story of other individuals who are defining the industry, one notable figure is Nobel Peace Prize Laureate Muhammad Yunus.[14]

ACHIEVING MACRO-LEVEL IMPACT THROUGH MICROFINANCE

Considered the founding father of microfinance, Muhammad Yunus influenced the banking industry and changed the way many do business. Some believe that he was born a changemaker, and others may credit his impact to a one-in-a-million chance occurrence. Yet Yunus never expected to go

---

13   "Corporate Social Responsibility (CSR)," Investopedia, accessed Oct. 16, 2020.

14   "Muhammad Yunus—Biographical," The Nobel Prize, accessed Jul. 14, 2020.

down the path he did at all. And it started with something so simple that anyone could have replicated it: with a small loan of $27.

Yunus was born in the village of Bathua in Bangladesh on June 28, 1940. He enjoyed a humble childhood. Between 1957–1960, he completed his BA in the Department of Economics at Dhaka University and later completed his MA in 1961. Yunus was later appointed as an economics lecturer at Chittagong College. When he was offered a Fulbright scholarship to study in the United States in 1965, he moved and obtained his PhD in economics from Vanderbilt University in 1969 before becoming an assistant professor of economics at Middle Tennessee State University. The professor, having been successful in his early career, lived a comfortable life.[15]

It was in the early 1970s that the winds of change began to blow. After the Liberation War of Bangladesh in 1971, the achievement of independence and subsequent birth of Bangladesh prompted Yunus to return to his home country in 1972 where he joined the Economics Department at the University of Chittagong.[16] He enjoyed a stable career, but the course of his life was shaken once more upon observing the famine of 1974 that consumed his country.[17]

During this time of suffering, Yunus didn't feel right teaching economics as if everything was fine when his country was

---

15   Ibid.

16   Ibid.

17   *Socialedge,* "Muhammad Yunus—Grameen Bank," Feb. 5, 2008, Video, 6:59.

starving to death. He wanted to feel closer to his people and took time to see the situation for himself. As he was going around the village, Yunus saw a woman in torn clothes sitting in front of a house making bamboo stools. The sight, with the cruel contrast between the beautiful stools and the backdrop of the torn-down house, sparked a sense of sorrow within him, and Yunus decided to interact with her. Curious about her craft, he asked her how much money she makes, who buys it, and how she markets her products. During their conversation, to his dismay, the woman revealed that she only made two pennies a day.[18]

Yunus was dumbfounded. He didn't understand how someone with her skill was making nearly less than enough to survive. Upon further conversation, the woman confided that she didn't have the twenty-five cents necessary for the bamboo material to make the stool, so she had to borrow the funds. The trader who lends her the money forces upon her a condition that she has to sell all the stools at the price that he decides. They leave her with only two cents from her sales.[19]

It was then that Yunus realized the truth and terrible ease of this cruel exploitation. The trader was not lending; rather, he had exploited this woman and turned her into a slave laborer. Overcome by a desire to change this, Yunus thought about ways that he could help this woman.

He realized that she would be saved if the root of the problem—the need for the lender—was eliminated. His simple

---

18   Ibid.
19   Ibid.

solution was to give the woman the money she needed for her bamboo stool business, thus ensuring she didn't have to borrow money and be exploited.[20]

"I was trying to do very little things. And I was not trying to persuade anybody to do anything. Just what I thought I could do, I tried to do that," Yunus stated.[21]

The next day, before taking his idea to action, Yunus went down to the village to see if other people were suffering from the same circumstances as the bamboo stool woman. He compiled a list of names who borrowed from the money lenders, leaving him with a list of forty-two women. The total amount borrowed from these women amounted to just $27. He couldn't believe that so little money could cause these people to suffer from such pain and humiliation. The problem was difficult, but the solution was so simple: By giving $27 to the forty-two people, Yunus could help them pay off the lenders and rid themselves of the exploitative debt.[22]

"It started with a little amount of money. So little that you can laugh at it. Total loan of $27 for forty-two people."[23]

---

20 Ibid.

21 *TEDx Talks,* "A History of Microfinance | Muhammad Yunus | TEDx-Vienna," Jan. 18, 2012, Video, 23:47.

22 Ibid.

23 TEDx Talks, A History of Microfinance, 23:47.

As he gave that $27 to the people, the happiness that it brought them moved him. "If you can make so many people so happy, with such a small amount of money, why shouldn't you do it more?" Yunus remarked with ease.[24]

By providing a series of small loans, he helped to create a series of sustainable small businesses. By helping those forty-two women escape exploitation, he created a sense of stability and comfort in the community. These women entrepreneurs shared their success with other women, effectively instigating this "multiplier effect" of impact (wherein an input in one area helps to stimulate growth and productivity in other areas of the community).[25]

This led him to create Grameen Bank and the concept of micro-loans—giving small loans of money to the poor who wouldn't otherwise be able to get any bank loans. The goal was to help unleash their entrepreneurial potential and create businesses that would allow them to raise themselves out of poverty.[26]

Not only was this lending concept revolutionary, but Grameen Bank itself was built on an entirely new model. According to Yunus, "I don't do very hard work. I'm an easy-going man. I just look at the conventional banks, how they do it. And once I learn how they do it, I just do the opposite."

24   Socialedge, Muhammad Yunus, 6:59.

25   "Multiplier Effect," Dictionary.com, accessed Oct. 22, 2020.

26   The Nobel Prize, Muhammad Yunus, Jul. 14, 2020.

He developed his bank for the poor upon a model that was opposite of everything that conventional banks functioned upon. "They go to the rich people; I go to the poor people. They go to men, so I decided to go to women," Yunus explains. They operate in big cities; Yunus goes to remote villages. Banks require collateral; Grameen Bank requires no such thing. Conventional banks are owned by rich people, so Grameen Bank is owned by the borrowers themselves. "We are not interested in the past of our borrowers. We are interested in the future of our borrowers."[27]

Despite the wonderful intentions, innovative method, and positive impact that he was creating, Yunus faced many challenges along the way. Notably, he was often met with apprehension owing to Grameen Bank's unconventional model of operating, where this active resistance of old thinking and combatting misguided norms drew many early criticisms from bankers.

In one meeting of bankers during the early tenth or eleventh year of operations, one banker confronted Yunus and told him, "Professor Yunus, you're not going to get away with this. You've made the whole banking system upside down."

Yunus honestly and amusingly replied that "Yes, that's exactly what I did because the banking system was standing on its head, so I'm trying to put it on its feet!"

Many people didn't agree with Yunus' idea of giving money to poor individuals, believing that money should only be lent

---

27   TEDx Talks, A History of Microfinance, 23:47.

to entrepreneurial people. Yet Yunus persisted in actively seeking out women in Bangladeshi towns and offering them these microloans. Even when the women tried to refuse his money, claiming that they'd never know how to use it, Yunus would keep chasing and explaining that they had the power to do it. He believed that it was the society that inflicted them with the sickness of self-doubt and wanted to build up their confidence to enable them to reach the potential he knew they could achieve.

In his view, just because one doesn't have confidence doesn't mean one lacks entrepreneurial ability. As Yunus holds the mindset that all people are entrepreneurs, he lends money to anyone and remains persistent in lending workers money to help them build confidence in themselves and their skills.[28]

Throughout his journey in microfinance, Yunus advocated his view of what he believed to be the missing category of business in the existing conceptual framework. "Conceptual framework gives you one type of business: to make money. That's the wrong interpretation of human beings. Human beings are not just money-making machines. Human beings are much bigger than just one-dimensional beings. They're multi-dimensional beings!"[29]

Over the past decades, Yunus has dedicated his life to responding to this missing piece himself. Rather than waiting for someone else to do something or following the norms, Yunus took it into his own hands to create a new form of

---

28 Ibid.
29 Ibid.

impact. Through his work in microfinance and the Grameen Bank, he redefined finance and tackled poverty to be the change he wanted to see.

Yunus' story is not only wholly inspiring, but also eye-opening. He created a business model out of a desire to create good through the power of business and credit, essentially going completely against the grain. The returns from this social approach are equally telling.

By adopting a unique mindset focused on generating value and social benefits, Muhammad Yunus was able to redefine an industry and revolutionize a new way of using business for positive social impact.

SOCIAL IMPACT—A DEFINITION

Muhammad Yunus, with just $27, was able to create revolutionary change. His contribution is just one example of the essence of positive social impact. But while his impact seems obvious, what exactly is "social impact?"

Professionals have disputed the term's possible definitions, some of which are explored by the Center for Social Impact Strategy, an action research center at the University of Pennsylvania's School of Social Policy and Practice. The center's founder, Peter Frumkin, defines it as "Any effort to solve complex social problems and create public value in the process."[30] Some other notable definitions include:

---

30 Ariel Schwartz, "What is Social Impact Anyways?" *The Center for Social Impact Strategy,* Aug. 30, 2017.

- "*Social impact can be defined as the net effect of an activity on a community and the well-being of individuals and families.*"[31]—Centre for Social Impact

- "*A significant, positive change that addresses a pressing social challenge.*"[32]—Michigan Ross Center for Social Impact

- "*Social impact is the effect an organization's actions have on the well-being of the community.*"[33]—Knowledge at Wharton High School

Bearing these definitions in mind, social impact, to me, is defined by any action that creates a change in the people and communities around you. While this is undoubtedly a more open definition, I prescribe to a similar belief of the Dean of UPenn's School of Social Policy & Practice, John L. Jackson, who believes that the importance and value of social impact come from the general concept behind it.[34]

In my view, social impact is not limited by the bounds of the measure of its impact nor the method by which one seeks to produce it. At its very foundation, we want to create social impact to benefit the greater good. Whether that's through a local act of kindness or on a national scale, all such actions are still impactful in their own way.

---

31 Ibid.

32 Ibid.

33 Ibid.

34 Ibid.

HISTORY OF NONPROFITS

When we think of social impact, the images of social work, charities, and non-governmental organizations (NGOs) are the first to come to mind. Indeed, since the origins of NGOs in the 1800s, the field has grown considerably and gained an admirable reputation to its name.

According to the Global Policy Forum, the first NGO was likely founded in 1839, known as the Anti-Slavery Society. This was the catalyst for similar organizations that grew out of wars, such as the Red Cross after the Franco-Italian War and Save the Children after World War I. Since then, NGO organizations have become the defining image as the promoters of social good, and for good reason. Their contributions are recognized around the world in addressing socio-economic issues, providing emergency aid, rallying for environmental change, and many others.[35]

In 2006, Peter Hall-Jones of the Global Policy Forum reported that the NGO sector is now the eighth largest in the world, valued at over $1 trillion a year and employing nineteen million paid workers and innumerable numbers of volunteers.[36] With the historical impact and contribution of NGO organizations in addressing society's social issues, the idea and image of social impact became synonymous with the nonprofit sector. Other social issues, such as the mistreatment of workers and environmental protection, were also imprinted upon government roles.

---

35 "The Rise and Rise of NGOs," Global Policy Forum, accessed Aug. 24, 2020.

36 Ibid.

Overall, what is imperative to note is that the current expansion and growth of the social impact industry is explosive and one which extends beyond the nonprofit sector.

AN EVOLVED ROLE OF SOCIAL IMPACT: BEYOND NONPROFITS

Especially in the past few decades, the role of social impact has shifted beyond the traditional sectors of government and nonprofits. New industries containing private sector traits have entered the social impact field. Some of these additions include:

- Microfinance engineered by Muhammad Yunus;
- Social entrepreneurship coined by Bill Drayton;
- and Impact investing pioneered by Ronald Cohen.

As we have discussed the story of microfinance in the story above, the following sections will relay the equally inspiring stories of social entrepreneurship and impact investing. In the ensuing section, I will tell the story of the latter sectors of social entrepreneurship and impact investing with stories just as powerful as that of Mr. Yunus.

RISE OF SOCIAL ENTREPRENEURSHIP

The term social entrepreneur was not known until 1980, when it was coined by the founding father of social entrepreneurship Bill Drayton. Yet before we understand the pioneer behind the term, it is important to recognize the historical context of the mid-to-late twentieth century.

***

"I have a dream," said Martin Luther King Jr. as he addressed the enormous gathering of civil rights marchers before him at the Lincoln Memorial. The crowd bustled with energy and respect as the words from the moving speech washed over the people. In the grand struggle for social justice and equal rights for Black Americans, this served as the defining point of the Civil Rights Movement that shook the American nation in the mid-1900s.[37] Indeed, the mid-to-late twentieth century saw a global awareness of civil unrest and disturbing inequality.

Amidst this bubbling cauldron of social issues, the need for social change was exacerbated. During these times, there emerged an international "citizens' sector" that sought to address such social problems along with the mobilization of not-for-profit organizations. Between 1968 and 1998, over 800,000 nonprofits were established.[38]

During this same time period, another solution was created which encompassed a way that would revolutionize the social impact and entrepreneurship sectors. Indeed, it took the form of an amalgamation of the two subjects into a new concept known as social entrepreneurship.

But in order to understand this dramatic development, we need to begin with another origin story; specifically, about

---

37   "Civil Rights Movement," History.com, accessed Nov. 23, 2020.

38   Peter Hall-Jones, Rise of NGOs, Aug. 24, 2020.

the founding father of social entrepreneurship Bill Drayton and how his idea revolutionized the realm of social impact.

***

In 1943, Bill Drayton was born in New York City to a family with a background as rich as his hometown. His mother was a cellist who had emigrated from Australia to the US, and his father an American explorer. The values of exploration, risk, and opportunity were pronounced. Bill's parents also came from families boasting backgrounds in civil rights, having been involved as abolitionists and women leaders.[39]

It was from this culmination of factors—his parents' free spirits, his family's dedication to public service, and Manhattan's diversity—that inspired his innovative and caring personality. Bill's journey of innovation would lead to a revolutionary development in the field of entrepreneurship and social impact.

As a child, Bill started small by undertaking entrepreneurial ventures such as managing a newspaper in fourth grade. He worked his way up to where he then created the Asia Society in high school, building it into the largest student organization in the school.[40]

Drayton pursued his bachelor's at Harvard. There, he founded the Ashoka Table, an interdisciplinary weekly forum

---

39   "Bill Drayton," All American Speakers, accessed Nov. 23, 2020.

40   "A Little Empathy Can Go a Long Way: The Bill Drayton Story," Ashoka United States, accessed Nov. 23, 2020.

offering guest appearances by prominent social leaders to provide students with the opportunity to ask them "how things worked."[41]

Drayton went on to work at McKinsey & Company as a consultant, which fed his interest in the workings of human institutions while providing valuable experience in dealing with public and private institutions. He was also an assistant administrator at the US Environmental Protection Agency (EPA) where he led administration-wide policy development.[42] Notably, he introduced the emissions trading reform that was revolutionary as a market-based approach to environmental regulation. It created the basis of global and US regulatory law extending to fields beyond the environment.

A colleague of Drayton's who worked with him at the EPA offered a telling comment about his innovative ideas and changemaking character: "Concepts that Bill was advocating twenty years ago, that were considered radical cave-ins by the environmental movement, are today advocated by nearly everybody as better ways to control pollution."[43]

While Drayton has always held the fundamental characteristics of entrepreneurship and social awareness, the explicit harmonization and coining of the phrase "social entrepreneurship" was not until a fateful trip that allowed him to tie all the pieces into a cohesive whole. This experience occurred

---

41 David Bornstein, "Changing the World on a Shoestring," *The Atlantic*, January 1998.

42 All American Speakers, "Bill Drayton," accessed Nov. 23, 2020.

43 David Bornstein, "Changing the World on a Shoestring," January 1998.

in 1972, when he traveled to India to help a man named Vinoba Bhave foster community development by redistributing land to create landowners who would better contribute to their communities. After successfully redistributing seven million acres of land, this experience became a turning point for Drayton. Upon witnessing the power of people in building up their communities through being provided the resources to do so, he recognized the power of entrepreneurial ideas to promote social change. Drayton then came upon the phrase "social entrepreneurship" and began to pursue that path for the rest of his career.[44]

The idea of creating a fellowship encompassing a community of social entrepreneurs and public innovators had been stewing in Drayton's mind since Harvard.[45] The rising movements in the US and social issues around the world were a wake-up call to Drayton about the dire state of the American and international community. For entrepreneurs like Drayton, when faced with a problem, they tend to ask, "What can I do?"

The solution came out of a recognition for the need now more than ever for social innovators and leaders—for this new breed of "social entrepreneurs." Encompassing those very values embedded in social entrepreneurship, Drayton created his own social organization called the Ashoka Fellowship dedicated to bringing together the world's leading

---

44   "Bill Drayton," Architects of Peace Foundation, accessed Nov. 23, 2020.

45   David Bornstein, "Changing the World on a Shoestring," January 1998.

individuals identified under this new concept of social entrepreneurship.[46]

Founded upon the belief that the power to create good for the world lies in its people, Drayton and a group of friends began to look for individuals who encompassed such values to be added to the Ashoka Fellowship. During their Christmas vacations in the late 1970s, they embarked on trips to India, Indonesia, and Venezuela, where they would look for candidates. It was a systematic process: They would invite those who had a reputation for public good and ask whether they knew anyone in their network who fit the definition of a social entrepreneur, someone driven by an innovative idea to address and resolve a global problem. They quickly compiled a collection of socially entrepreneurial candidates. "We came away thinking, 'Boy, these people are something,' and seeing that it was the right time to do this," Drayton noted.[47]

This early process was facilitated entirely by volunteers, donations, and Drayton's own pocket. By 1981, they compiled hundreds of people fit for Ashoka's first selection panel and distilled their unique traits, electing some among them to the Ashoka Fellowship. The impact and dedication Drayton brought to his work did not go unnoticed; he won the MacArthur Fellowship in 1984, which allowed him to continue growing Ashoka, raising millions from private donors and foundations.[48]

---

46   All American Speakers, "Bill Drayton," accessed Nov. 23, 2020.

47   David Bornstein, "Changing the World on a Shoestring," January 1998.

48   Ibid.

The Ashoka Fellowship and the concept of social entrepreneurship rose dramatically. Ashoka fellows began becoming elected in countries around the world, and by 1988, one hundred fellows had been elected in four countries, building the foundation of a community.[49]

The decade of 1990 saw a blossom of growth from what had been a budding organization. Its presence, value, and importance were disseminated across the globe: At home, prestigious institutions such as Harvard Business School established social entrepreneurship programs fitting with the new sector. As Drayton commented, "When we started, there was no word for this field. If you don't have a word, it tells you that not much is going on. But today, everyone wants to be a social entrepreneur. Universities all over the world have courseware on the subject. That's new."[50]

As the late 1990s rolled around, one thousand social entrepreneurs had been selected into the fellowship. In 2005, having surpassed their goal of establishing social entrepreneurship in the public realm, Ashoka shifted their focus to promoting a vision known as "Everyone a Changemaker" (EACH). This would continue construction of a world where everyone is aware of how they can create change to shape a better world.[51]

This idea of social entrepreneurship truly revolutionized both the impact and entrepreneurship sectors alike. To this

49 "Ashoka's History," Ashoka India, accessed Nov. 23, 2020.

50 How Do You Change the World? Become a Social Entrepreneur, Interview by Scott London, *Scott London,* March 2012.

51 "Ashoka Envisions a World in Which Everyone is a Changemaker," Ashoka United States, accessed Nov. 23, 2020.

Drayton makes the case that supporting these social entrepreneurs is a better investment than simple philanthropy, as Ashoka Fellows can bring sustainable change to their communities, improving them beyond what the means of a simple pay check. Essentially, this is reminiscent of the following Chinese saying: "Give a man a fish and you feed him for a day; teach a man to fish and you feed him for a lifetime."[52] In the same way, Ashoka Fellows create a system-changing, enduring impact beyond what money can solve and, in the process, bring the community together in lifting each other. The fellows themselves would recruit thousands of other local changemakers to contribute to their cause and inspire another generation of entrepreneurs.[53]

Bill Drayton famously said that "Social entrepreneurs don't want to help. They want to change the world."[54] And through Ashoka, he has done just that. His idea of social entrepreneurs founded upon changemaking behavior that defies human's innate aversion to change is revolutionary. The Ashoka Fellowship, through the simple act of putting the value back with the people, is a seemingly simple concept that has such fantastic rewards. The growth of social entrepreneurship from an unknown term to something taught in the curriculum of the nation's most prestigious institutions is nothing short of remarkable.

---

52 "The Meaning and Origin of the Expression: Give a Man a Fish, and You Feed Him for a Day; Show Him How to Catch Fish, and You Feed Him for a Lifetime," Phrase Finder, accessed Aug. 13, 2020.

53 Scott London, How Do You Change the World?, Interview

54 "Social Entrepreneurs Don't Want to Help. They Want to Change the World.", Interview by Parallel Worlds, *Parallel Worlds,* (n.d.)

Today, social entrepreneurship continues to grow and touch the lives of people who seek to find innovative and entrepreneurial ways to solve societal issues. It has had a profound impact on people around the world, guiding their paths while providing a memorable story of remarkable change.

RISE OF IMPACT INVESTING

Another growing field in the social impact realm is a harmonization of the investment components of finance coupled with the goals from social impact known as impact investing. This is a type of venture capitalism that invests in companies, organizations, and funds that have the intention to create a measurable social or environmental benefit in addition to a financial return.[55] It has grown in popularity due to financial investors seeking purpose and meaning in their lives. With recent studies showing that impact investments have significant returns, other investors were encouraged to consider social impact startups. Worldwide, impact investment organizations manage over $502 billion of assets, which is nearly double the amount from the year before.[56]

But similar to the concept of social entrepreneurship, this industry of impact investing was not known until only a few decades ago when Sir Ronald Cohen pioneered the initiatives of impact investing. Cohen carries a plethora of accolades, most notably known as the Chairman of the Global Steering Group for Impact Investment and the co-founder director of

---

55   "Impact Investing," Global Impact Investing Network, accessed Jul. 13, 2020.

56   Abhilash Mudaliar and Hannah Dithrich, *Sizing the Impact Investing Market* (New York: The GIIN, 2019)

Social Finance UK, USA, and Israel. In 2012, he received the Rockefeller Foundation's Innovation Award for innovation in social finance. Despite these awards and accomplishments, similar to Yunus and Drayton, Cohen also built his way up in a meaningful and inspiring way.[57]

***

Cohen was born in Egypt to a Jewish family after the service crisis. At the age of eleven, he traveled with his family to Britain as refugees with a suitcase and ten Egyptian pounds each. Despite the odds against them in this new country, his father supported him greatly when he was young, which motivated him to not let the effort his father gave to provide him with opportunities go to waste. Essentially, he adopted a pay-it-forward attitude and ultimately rose to the top of his class, graduating from renowned institutions like Oxford and Harvard Business School.[58]

In school, the prevailing culture was the idea that "big is beautiful." While each of Cohen's student peers wanted to join a big company, he was first interested in venture capital when he heard a speech from one of the first venture capitalists who taught at Harvard Business School. He was inspired by the industry and wanted to get involved. "One of the reasons I became a venture capitalist was to help people improve their lives," he explained.[59]

---

57 "Bio," Sir Ronald Cohen, accessed Aug. 10, 2020.

58 *Forbes,* "From Refugee to Venture Capitalist to Social Impact Pioneer | Forbes," Aug. 6, 2018, Video, 5:00.

59 Ibid.

As the industry was still developing in Europe, Cohen became a trailblazer for the venture capital industry there, seeking to create a fairer and more prosperous future for all. Realizing that entrepreneurship didn't just have to be an American phenomenon, he sought to bring it to Europe, where you had a shot of providing jobs to Britain's significant population of the unemployed.[60]

At the age of twenty-six, Cohen founded Apax Partners, a then venture capital firm. This early and respectable endeavor provided him with many valuable lessons. First, Cohen believes that uncertainty is a friend of the entrepreneur and the venture capitalist, and that great success can only be achieved by turning uncertainty into your friend. He imbues the wisdom from starting early in his book *The Second Bounce of the Ball*, where he provides the message to "Start young, think big, and stick with it."[61]

- By starting young and getting into a new field ahead of others, you'll get experience in it before anyone else and become a pioneer, which can translate to having a good shot in leading the field in the future.

- On thinking big, Cohen reflects the well-known idea of having big dreams as those ambitious goals are what will lead you down the path for growth and innovation.

- Finally, the "stick with it" idea addresses the times that you will undoubtedly question whether you are on the

60 Ibid.

61 The Impact Revolution: Reshaping Capitalism, Interview by DLD Sync, *DLD Sync*, Oct. 5, 2020.

right path. At these moments, if you're not reaching your destination, you simply need to adjust.

Throughout his career, Cohen's values and aims greatly shifted. While he was creating impact in supporting entrepreneurs through venture capital, he wanted to do more. The entrepreneurs that he was backing came from simple backgrounds and did not deal with the social issues he was passionate about, such as poverty. And as entrepreneurship and capital grew, Cohen noticed that wealth inequality actually expanded and social issues continued to spread.[62]

Cohen didn't want his epitaph to read "Delivered a 13 percent rate of return for fifteen years." He found there to be no sense in accumulating more money; rather, he wanted to see if he could make a dent in solving social issues. In 2005, Cohen left venture capital and moved on to do what he deemed to be more effective in creating positive impact.[63]

After the 2008 financial crisis, it became clear that the system itself was creating social problems. Cohen realized that we needed to innovate, to enable social organizations to grow in the same way that businesses grow. "If you can redirect capital flows to improve people's lives, you begin to resolve problems that government alone can't resolve," he explained.[64]

He began looking at poverty and how our system deals with it. With his experience in investing, Cohen realized that we

---

62 Forbes, "From Refugee to Venture Capitalist," YouTube.

63 Ibid.

64 Ibid.

never thought about bringing investment capital to those that want to improve the lives of others and the planet. The idea of bringing finance and social expertise to connect social entrepreneurs with capital markets was born. This became a mission for Cohen, which led him to develop the first social impact bond in the world that used investor money to fund intervention programs for released prisoners in the UK with great success. Within five years, reoffending rates decreased by 9 percent, and the money savings for the government was paid back to investors.[65]

This was, in essence, one of the first demonstrations of impact investing. It entails the optimization of risk, returns, and impact, using financing and investing techniques to support those who seek to do good in the world. "Impact investment is about giving people a chance. People don't want charity; they want a chance." Cohen stresses that, in our current society, we can no longer optimize risk and return alone. It is essential to bring a social and environmental purpose.[66]

"Achieving impact. That's the future."

Cohen believes that there's a revolution happening, and that if you have a higher mission, then you can inspire people to rise to even greater efforts. "I would like my legacy to be something that inspired and helped the impact revolution to take place," Cohen confessed.[67]

---

65 Ibid.

66 Ibid.

67 Ibid.

According to Cohen, the world is shifting to one of risk, return, and impact. He believes that the most successful businesses of the future will have high impact integrity: "Within twenty years, every business will need to incorporate impact in its business model to ensure success and survive. It's what consumers, investors, and employees are demanding. They will deliver impact across the world."[68]

Indeed, having pioneered the industry of impact investing, Cohen has inspired generations of people to drive the future through impact and profit.

TRANSITIONING TO PURPOSE-DRIVEN ACTIONS

Our world is constantly changing. As we've seen through the transition of business roles in society as well as the emerging social impact industries, this Impact Revolution is here.

According to *Forbes*, "Its reverberations are being felt across executive boardrooms, foundation offices, and startups. It's fundamentally shifting the way investments are made, policies are penned, funds are endowed, and careers are chosen."[69]

As our world changes, we must adapt with it. With growing awareness over the social and environmental issues plaguing modern society, the growth in the social impact industries make them all-the-more valuable.

---

68   DLD Sync, Impact Revolution, Interview by DLD Sync.

69   *Forbes,* "The Social Impact Revolution is Here | Forbes," Jun. 25, 2018, Video, 2:32.

While the shift in business is impressive, these developments in social impact have also provided any person with the unique abilities to create impact in their everyday lives, an observation upon which I build my theory of "Everyday Impact."

Statistics from the Global Entrepreneurship Monitor describe forty-one percent of Gen Z who want to pursue an entrepreneurial career path, with sixty-four percent saying they consider inspiring work an essential part of any job.[70] Such numbers indicate an eagerness in young people to support social causes, especially considering the growth of course selection for high school and early post-secondary classes that can generate a social impact. Veritably, the act of holding social impact as a value for your career is an impactful decision.

Through this book, not only do I hope to show the different ways that you can create impact in industries and entrepreneurship, but that small acts can also be an amazing tool for positive change. I hope to provide ways in which anyone can create a positive change in their society and to show how there is a changemaker in each of us.

---

70 Entrepreneur Staff, "41 Percent of Gen Z-ers Plan to Become Entrepreneurs (Infographic)," *Entrepreneur*, Jan. 15, 2019.

CHAPTER 2

WHY NOW?

———

A PERSONAL INTRODUCTION TO SOCIAL IMPACT

I have always been enamored by tailored suits and corporate high-rises. As a child, I was enraptured by the prospect of working in a futuristic office, sitting at a desk next to a glass wall offering a panoramic view of the bustling city below.

Yet despite my interest in corporate life, growing up, the image of working in business was nothing short of intimidating. My Chinese parents would tell me about jobs that made the most money, effectively promoting the idea that business was the industry where the "big money" could be found. Coupled with the cutthroat image of corporations and businessmen as portrayed by media, my perception of business became associated with the image of that evil corporate mastermind: One hand holding a suitcase filled with cash and the fingers in the other rubbing together in that ubiquitous sign of *ka-ching*.

I wanted to make my parents proud, and I would need a lot of money to give them and myself the lifestyle that I wanted. But did I have to sell my soul to do so? Did my success have to come at the expense of others?

My world changed in grade ten. In the spring semester, during my fourth-period business class, we learned about the concept of CSR. As we studied different cases and examples of corporations giving back to their communities, I became fascinated by this side of business that I never knew. The previous image I had gradually shifted as I began to see how corporations and business operations could do more than just earn a profit. A spark of hope rose within me with this discovery as I realized that it was possible to bridge my altruistic self with my interest in business.

My interest in this novel discovery exploded in grade eleven. When researching courses, I discovered a unique program known as the Foundation for Student Science and Technology Online Research Co-op.[71] Recognizing the importance of research for post-secondary and lured by its academic rigor, I enthusiastically applied.

When I was accepted into the program, I expressed my desire and interest to explore CSR in my research. In the past, students were assigned university professors as mentors and made to write a research paper, making the program more geared toward STEM (Science, Technology, Engineering, and

---

71 "Online Research Coop Program," The Journal of Student Science and Technology, accessed Dec. 18, 2020.

Math) students. With my niche interest, it took a much longer time for the foundation to find a suitable mentor for me.

Nevertheless, it was well worth the wait. On a seemingly inconspicuous day in mid-October, I received a message on Slack, the virtual workplace that the program used to facilitate communication, explaining that I was paired with the executive director of OneChild, an NGO advocating against child sex trafficking. Instead of the usual research paper, I was tasked with creating a social return on investment (SROI) report documenting the economic and social return of preventing a child from falling victim to sex trafficking. Not only was this the first NGO collaboration with the co-op program, but this SROI was the first of its kind in the world.

It would be an understatement to say that I was overwhelmed. Safe to say, I was *floored*.

The announcement fell upon a stupefied face. Here I was, the personification of familiarity and constancy, now thrown into the fire of novelty and risk. This was a level of scholarship unbeknownst to me, and the risks of not measuring up to an NGO's standards formed a doubtful thought bubble within my mind questioning, "Can I really do this?"

But as someone who never gives up on something before trying it first, I felt compelled to conduct preliminary research on child sex trafficking to gain an understanding of the issue. Reading about the manipulative emotional conditioning used to trap children in the cycle of exploitation filled me with indignation. Learning about the prevalence of sex trafficking, I was haunted by the fact that anyone can become a victim.

However, I was lucky enough to be blessed with this voice to speak out and the freedom to take action. I had the means to change an unacceptable reality. My previous concerns became eclipsed by an exigent desire to contribute to OneChild's cause, turning that uncertain thought bubble into a motivated voice asking, "How can I do this?"

Over the next few months, I dedicated my time to research and outreach. After three hundred and twenty-five hours of number-crunching and writing, I created the first-ever SROI report identifying the economic cost of child sex trafficking in Canada to stress the benefit of funding prevention. With the printed paper in hand, I delighted in the knowledge that my work would help prevent future children from falling into a lifetime of suffering. I was overcome by that indescribable but distinct euphoria of finding your *joie de vivre*. It was the end of my co-op, but this discovery of my altruistic passion inspired the start of my aspiration for social impact.

My goal solidified in grade twelve. As university application season rolled around and I was forced to consider my future career goals, I realized that my desire to enact positive social change was my greatest strength. Without conscious intention, the majority of my university application essays revolved around my desire to serve and achieve social impact in my future.

The early summer of 2020 then presented a unique opportunity to reaffirm and pursue this passion. When the COVID-19 pandemic forced people to stay inside, I made the most of my time by seeking networking opportunities. During my time in isolation, I met a variety of professionals from all different backgrounds and walks of life. The experience of speaking with them one-on-one and receiving their mentorship was life-changing. They would provide me with invaluable life and career advice, all while supporting me in my social impact goals. Despite being distinguished professionals, their desire to help young students like me was empowering.

In sharing their knowledge, wisdom, and experiences, the mentors I've had the pleasure of meeting during the quarantine have changed my life. In this way, I felt empowered to do the same. Tying this desire to give back and my passion for social impact, I realized that the best way for me to share the insights I've learned and inspire other changemakers is to express this message through a public platform.

After these years, my passion for social impact still burns strong. The only difference? My voice that seeks to inspire others to strive for social impact in their own lives yearns to be heard. And this book is the very outlet by which I will broadcast my message.

Undeniably, the concept of social impact has changed and defined my life at a time when I felt lost. In the same way, I seek to share my passion with you to provide you with the same opportunity to grow through impact and purpose.

GREETINGS FROM YOUR PERSONAL GUIDE

As your guide along this journey of impact, it is only appropriate that I formally introduce myself.

Greetings! I'm Erin, a Wharton Class of 2024 student and bubble tea connoisseur, but most proudly an avid volunteer and passionate advocate for social impact.

My ultimate hope is to inspire within all readers a profound sense of helping others beyond the notion that it's the "right thing to do," but also because the benefits and fulfilment from a life of service and purpose are beyond any self-interested dream that one could have.

THE PURPOSE OF EVERYDAY IMPACT

My hope for this book is to inspire a new generation of changemakers. To show that your life is in your hands. To not fit yourself into the status quo, but to reach beyond it. To not settle for personal gain, but to pursue meaning and purpose in changing the lives of others and leaving your legacy.

The times are changing, and there is no better time than now to appreciate the value of this message.

So let us begin with a brief history of how social impact has evolved since the old economy.

THE IMPACT EVOLUTION SINCE THE OLD ECONOMY: HISTORY VS. TODAY

The roots of social responsibility in corporations date back centuries, with many of its roots coming from corporate philanthropy. In the nineteenth century, Andrew Carnegie—one of America's most renowned businessmen—promoted the notion of supporting social causes and dedicating oneself to philanthropy in his book the *Gospel of Wealth*.[72] John D. Rockefeller, another individual with renowned status, took inspiration from Carnegie, using his business and wealth to donate more than half a billion dollars.

The year 1914 saw the creation of the first community foundation by Frederick Goff, a well-known banker in Cleveland. He founded the Cleveland Foundation as a trustee of the Cleveland Trust Company to empower the community by accepting gifts from multiple donors who could collectively better assess the needs and provide responses to the community.[73]

The 1940s marked a pivotal development, as businesses themselves—rather than solely their owners or shareholders—could begin to support charities. The title of "father of CSR" is often given to Howard Bowen, an American economist and Grinnell College president, owing to his book *Social Responsibilities of the Businessman*.[74] In it, he explicitly promoted the connection between the responsibility of corporations

---

72   Andrew Carnegie, *The Gospel of Wealth* (New York: Carnegie Corporation of New York), 1-48.

73   "The World's First Permanent but Flexible 'Community Savings Account'," Foundation of Change, accessed Aug. 2, 2020.

74   Howard R. Bowen, *Social Responsibilities of the Businessman* (Iowa City: University of Iowa Press), 1-207.

and society. Published in 1953, it was pivotal for business ethics and responsiveness to societal stakeholders.

In the 1970s, CSR was further highlighted when the Committee for Economic Development formally recognized the concept of the "social contract" between business and society.[75] It was based on the idea that businesses only exist and function because the public provided their consent. Therefore, business is obligated to serve society's needs constructively and effectively.

From then on, numerous models of CSR would be developed, but all of which had the same idea of doing more on a social scale and promoting good for a business' surrounding society. Early adopters of CSR included companies such as The Hershey Company that built civic centers, cultural institutions, and other community facilities.[76]

Today, we know the values of ethics and social responsibility as integral to the goals and functioning of organizations. From Lego Braille Bricks to pledges from corporations to switch to 100 percent sustainable materials in packaging, many organizations are "turning a new page" as they begin to incorporate social value into their operations.[77] Indeed, this progressive trend toward social responsibility is undoubtedly an admirable and positive movement. Over the past few

---

75   "Corporate Social Responsibility: A Brief History," Association of Corporate Citizenship Professionals, accessed Aug. 4, 2020.

76   Ibid.

77   "Introducing Lego Braille Bricks," Lego Braille Bricks, accessed Aug. 6, 2020.

decades, this importance of social responsibility has developed into a social norm.

AN EVOLVING SOCIAL NORM

As introduced in the previous chapter, the increasing demand for CSR has given rise to numerous industries and purpose-driven organizations. Such social purpose corporations include social enterprises and benefit corporations, otherwise known as B Corps. Today, the number of B Corps has exceeded 2,750 compared to the mere 82 B Corps in 2007.[78, 79]

The influence of social impact has presented itself uniquely in education. According to the Saïd Business School at Oxford University, "The Social Impact sector is a rapidly changing environment that is leading innovation and ground-breaking change almost daily." Consistent with an increased interest among millennials to use their skills toward benefiting a cause and careers with purpose, many MBA students at Oxford Saïd are interested in industries including Fintech, Edtech, Impact Investing, and Impact Consulting.[80]

Consumers are showing similar trends through their interest in socially responsible purchasing. According to the Center for Social Impact Strategy from the University of Pennsylvania, 90 percent of millennials would switch to a

78 Rapid Transition Alliance, "The Decline of the Single Bottom Line and the Growth of B-Corps," *Rapid Transition Alliance,* Aug. 16, 2019.

79 "How Did the B Corp Movement Start?" B Corporation, accessed Aug. 6, 2020.

80 "Social-Impact Industry Support," Saïd Business School, accessed Aug. 7, 2020.

cause-branded product when given the choice between two brands with equal quality and price. Further, 51 percent of global consumers are willing to pay extra for goods and services that are committed to positive social and environmental impact.[81]

Deloitte has also conducted studies that found trends in the shift to social responsibility. In the past 10 years, they have reported a noticeable shift in the way that public companies think about the social impact of their businesses as a strategic driver of value. Their research shows that companies from all different industries have adopted and utilized a social impact mindset to differentiate their products, explore new markets, attract younger talent, and transform regulatory relationships. As the article notes, "Social impact has evolved from a pure PR play to an important part of corporate strategy to protect and create value. It is a trend driven largely by millennial consumers and enabled by social media tools that have taken accountability and transparency to new heights."[82]

TAKEAWAYS

In many ways, the world is changing for the better. Accordingly, as citizens and contributing members of society, we must adapt and do our part to reflect these same positive changes.

---

81 The Center for Social Impact Strategy, "What is Social Impact Anyways?" *Social Impact Fundamentals*, Aug. 30, 2017.

82 "Driving Corporate Growth Through Social Impact: Four Corporate Archetypes to Maximize Your Social Impact," Deloitte, accessed July 19, 2020.

Fortunately, we are already seeing a shift toward altruism as a social norm. Simultaneously with the adoption of CSR values and purpose-driven expectations, we see growing instances of people conducting actions in both their professional and daily lives to promote a better society.

We have seen the rise of impactful initiatives such as the Pay It Forward movement, which encouraged people to conduct three unprompted good deeds for three different people. The idea was to ask for nothing in return except that the people you helped could "pay it forward" by doing well to someone else. This seemingly simple movement has spread worldwide, inspiring a book and a film.[83] Another notable example includes Operation Beautiful, a project consisting of sticking post-it notes with positive, uplifting messages in public places to inspire others to feel better about themselves and pass the message along to someone else.[84]

Especially since the COVID-19 pandemic hit, a stronger sense of community was fostered, inspiring a "we're all in this together" kind of attitude. This represents a new trend beyond big business, to true empowerment of individuals in doing great things for others and shaping the community around them.

83 "The Pay it Forward Movement," The Melvin and Bren Simon Foundation, accessed Aug. 8, 2020.

84 "Operation Beautiful," Operation Beautiful, accessed Aug. 8, 2020.

THE INDUSTRIES OF THE FUTURE AND WHY WE NEED "EVERYDAY IMPACT"

While organizations and people are stepping up to the challenge, this has created another problem. We live in an age where media inundates us with information about gargantuan contributions such as billions in donations that can cause us to feel disheartened.

But through this book, I hope to prove that we can and should make a difference in our society, and how seemingly small or simple actions can mean so much more than you think. I seek to empower people to understand the potential in themselves to do good for others and, in the process, for themselves.

This book will explore the increasingly relevant intersections of business and altruism, of normal careers and innovation, to show how you can go above-and-beyond to leave a lasting legacy. It explores the intersections of purpose and profit, tackling key themes of what motivates people to work and how we can leverage passion and impact into helping us get to the next level. Most importantly, this book explores the intersections of what I like to call the 3 I's of Meaningful Change: the Inspiration of the Past, Impact of the Present, and the Innovation of the Future. In my book, I analyze how these three principles are manifested in the stories of impact-oriented people and explain how the reader can apply these principles to their own life to make a meaningful impact and change, both externally to others as well as internally to themselves.

PREVIEW + FRAMEWORK

This book can be compared to a collection of stories. The details of others' personal experiences from primary and secondary interviews are what's used to promote the fundamental ideas and themes of the corresponding chapter. These chapters all contain personal narratives, research, and summaries to provide evidence and context to the information.

Fitting with its purpose as a guide to one's journey of social impact, the 3 I's are meant to serve as a guide; beginning with helping you find your passion, then seeing how you can transform that to impact, and finally how you can differentiate yourself in the impact you create.

LOOKING INTO THE FUTURE

This will not be your typical book covering the sole success stories of society's wealthiest or most popular. While there may be some famous names you might recognize, the bulk of stories are told by people no more different than you and me. With that being said, it proves how these principles and insights that you'll soon read can be applicable and practiced by anyone.

As we prepare to embark on this journey, I would implore you to think critically about the stories you'll read. Rather than seeing them as simple biographies, consider the deeper meanings and methods behind each changemaker's actions and take inspiration from them.

Be conscious about which ideas resonate with you and determine how the principles of the 3 I's can be uniquely applied to your life.

These are stories of everyday impact, and I hope that they will help you to embark on your own journey of impact.

PART II

INSPIRATION

CHAPTER 3

FROM HARDSHIPS TO INSPIRATION

——

Turn your wounds into wisdom.

—OPRAH WINFREY[85]

FROM REFUGEE TO ADVOCACY—AHLAM'S STORY

One's childhood can build the road of their adult life.

For Ahlam, the reality of her childhood was a harrowing map that, under the circumstances, would have led her down a dangerous path. She was born into an extremely conservative family in conflict-ridden Palestine which was under Zionist occupation. In her childhood, Ahlam could not share the same innocent memories of summer lemonade stands and

---

85 Larry Kim, "19 Short Inspirational Quotes for Overcoming Adversity," *Inc.com*, May 28, 2015.

park adventures with friends that most children in Western society had. Simply stated, she did not have a normal, much less enjoyable childhood than most.

"I remembered the Israel soldiers attacking my house and our neighbors after midnight," Ahlam recalls with a sad, faraway look. "There was a curfew and a lack of food, electricity, and medication. I did not have proper access to the institutions: I was suffering from tooth pain and migraine for one month during curfew, and the soldier did not allow my father to take me to the doctor. I saw them beating my father in the street, threatening him that he would be arrested if he went out again. My mother removed my teeth at home."

Ahlam confesses that her childhood experiences put her in a constant state of insecurity. Burdened with nightmares even now, when she sees a police officer in the street, she remembers every single event from her childhood. Engrossed in the memory, Ahlam told me her story.

"I am a witness of Israeli wars and massacres of Sabra and Shatila. I have waited for hours at the checkpoints to have permission from soldiers to visit Jerusalem. Sometimes, I am forced to return home without either visiting my lovely city or practicing my religion."

"I did not have a childhood like many children in the world. I still remembered when I was four years old, crying in the car at Israel's security checkpoints. My mom was doing her best to make me quiet down to avoid the soldier hearing my voice, as that would cause her more problems.

"I saw how the soldiers made my father stand in the hot and cold weather at the checkpoints for a long time. I saw my parents walking between trees, hiding from the soldiers for hours to bring our food and medicine."

"I was there when my late father left home at 4:00 a.m. to reach his work by 8:00 a.m. despite the distance from home to his workplace being only five kilometers. I saw my relatives delivering their baby at the checkpoints without any medical support; I saw the soldiers laughing while they were punishing my father and others."

As Ahlam finished her story, the harrowing truth of her childhood stuck like a rock in one's throat, simply impossible to swallow. Despite the circumstances being stacked against her, despite the oppression and trauma, Ahlam rejected this path of destruction that her childhood had constructed.

"When you're facing such a situation where you feel you are a victim, you can act in two ways: You either hate society and act negatively, or you recognize that you do something different. I chose to do something different."

PAST, PRESENT, AND FUTURE—THE RESEARCH BEHIND ONE'S EXPERIENCES AND ITS IMPACT ON THE FUTURE

The effect of one's upbringing has severe implications on their future, and numerous research studies have provided evidence of the relationship between past experiences and present actions.

In a study by Orit E. Tykocinski and Andreas Ortmann, they documented the influence of past experiences on present perceptions, emotions, decisions, and goals. As they note, many behavioral science practitioners prescribe to the belief that "nothing predicts future behavior like past behavior." The authors analyze how past experiences may improve judgements and decisions, outlining three main ways that our psychological makeup is shaped by our pasts and its subsequent effect on present circumstances:[86]

1. We all carry "unfinished business," and while our goals and circumstances may have changed, those unfinished activities, obligations, and relationships are no longer optimal.

2. Past experiences can serve as reference points to compare options, experiences, and achievements in the present, which evoke emotions of elation, counterfactual thoughts, or regret.

3. Consequences of past choices and actions can be powerful determinants of current resources. For example, a past failure may elicit feelings of insecurity.

The article makes clear that while our past may not have an insignificant impact on our present, we as autonomous beings must take advantage of our capacity to learn from the

---

86   Orit E. Tykocinski and Andreas Ortmann, "The Lingering Effects of Our Past Experiences: The Sunk-Cost Fallacy and the Inaction-Inertia Effect," *Social and Personality Psychology Compass* 5, no. 9 (2011): 653-664.

past rather than automatically resigning to a reflection of its shadows. It's important to look forward to the opportunities ahead with motive in mind.

So while the impact of our past experiences is great, the important thing is not to get swept up in them, but to use them as tools to better and shape our identities. For true strength lies not just in surviving an experience but taking from it the strength to do better upon oneself.

THE TURNING POINT—HOW AHLAM TURNED TO IMPACT

Rather than remaining bitter and cursing the unfairness of her past forever, Ahlam sought to actively make a difference. This harrowing past was what led Ahlam to strive to create a world where people would not have to go through what she suffered.

Ahlam became a part of the political movement in her country. As an advocate for human and women's rights, she founded the Arab governance center and contributed to numerous women and youth empowerment programs to help young girls who were in a similar position that she was in the past overcome their challenges.

In 1991, during the Iraqi crisis and Gulf War in Jordan, Ahlam worked as the head of the department for a religious program. As many refugees were searching for a safe place in Jordan, she was helping people daily, providing them with cash and psychological assistance as well as vocational training to be prepared for the labor market. The feeling of doing something greater than business motivated her, and she loved her work.

In December of 2019, Ahlam moved to Canada and attended York University for her PhD. As a part of her scholarship, she currently serves as the teacher's assistant for the Human Rights and Equity Department. Even in Canada, Ahlam supports and advocates for international students, specifically for those who can't pay their tuition fees or rent an apartment. She is also involved with Change.org for advocacy where she signs petitions and, taking advantage of innovation and the technical landscape, frequently raises awareness for social issues on her social media.

Ahlam continues to embrace innovation by finding different ways to communicate and advocate. During the summer of the 2020 COVID-19 pandemic, Ahlam adapted to the circumstances and transitioned her teaching online, hosting weekly Zoom sessions for her students.

To conclude, Ahlam shared three messages to three of the fundamental groups of our society:

"My message to all is that love is the key to life. My message to the government is to include the volunteerism culture in the students' curriculum during the early stages of school. My message for students is to see the whole picture and try to have additional goals in your life outside of yourself to support society and make changes in our world."

AN IMMIGRANT CHILD'S IMPACTFUL UPBRINGING

The experience of being impacted by your childhood is ubiquitous. In my case, my relationship with my Chinese heritage reinforced the power of cultural upbringing.

I was born in Canada to a Chinese couple who had newly immigrated to the North American country. At the time, my parents were humbly renting a single room in someone else's house. Having not yet found a stable footing for themselves, they realized their environment was not the way they wanted their child to grow up. I was thus brought back to China to be raised by my grandparents until I could rejoin my parents at their newly financed apartment six years later.

Throughout my life, I bore witness to the immense struggles that my family suffered. Since my father couldn't find a job in the small town in which we were located, he was forced to work a night shift job in a town over one hundred kilometers away. When I was just about to start high school, the company that my mother worked for shut down, and she was left without a job. She spent a year trying to find employment, even working for half a year in the US before securing a job in downtown Toronto, one hundred thirty-two kilometers away from our home. So began an arduous routine of twelve-hour workdays and daily four-hour commutes.

With both parents working in the Toronto region, the question of why we couldn't simply move houses frequently crossed my mind. Yet each time my parents met my inquiry with a simple smile and a subsequent question of whether I was happy in my current school. Of course, after having found my friend group and being fully comfortable with the community, I was more than content in this familiar environment. To my parents, hearing that was all the answer they needed.

We never did move closer to their work, but in my school and town, I flourished.

It was only after I became older that I understood the extent of my family's sacrifice, inspiring a lifetime of altruism within me. I came to understand the importance of sacrifice and helping others from a young age. Reflecting on my upbringing has allowed me to solidify my understanding of the significant influence that one's upbringing can have in shaping the person one becomes.

So I urge you to look within yourself, recall your past, and reflect on its connection to you now. Fully appreciate how far you've come and the role that previous events have had in shaping who you are now.

Just as it is imperative to have a goal for the future, it is equally important to reflect on where you came from and learn from your upbringing. Often, what can be just as powerful as experiencing hardship yourself is seeing others go through that suffering. The desire to prevent that from happening again is life-shaping.

FIGHTING AGAINST THE GUN

Ahlam's story has incredible circumstances unique to herself. In the same vein, my story is also one with situations and relationships that no one else can replicate. However, this trend of how we reach impact through past experiences is echoed in the story of renowned youth advocate Malala Yousafzai.

Malala is known around the world as an education advocate and the youngest recipient of the Nobel Peace Prize. But her fight for girls was born out of an intense struggle and near-death experience.[87]

Malala was born in Mingora, Pakistan, where the birth of a baby girl wasn't a cause for celebration. Her father, however, was determined for her to have the same opportunities as any boy. Growing up, Malala loved school, and her father was a teacher who ran a girls' school.

When the Taliban took control of her village, they banned girls from having access to education. Angered by the injustice, Malala spoke out and became a public advocate for girls' right to education. Her admirable and selfless endeavor placed a red target on her head.[88]

In October 2012, a gunman boarded Malala's bus as she was returning from school. After asking "Who is Malala?" he shot her on the left side of her head. The attack garnered international attention, and when Malala awoke from her hospital in Birmingham, England, ten days later, the international community was praying for her recovery.[89]

---

87 "Malala's Story," Malala Fund, accessed Oct. 9, 2020.

88 Ibid.

89 Ibid.

The road to recovery was not an easy one for the young girl, and she endured months of surgeries and rehabilitation. Their family had made a new home in the UK, but Malala wasn't ready to settle; she wanted to do more.[90]

> "It was then I knew I had a choice: I could live a quiet life, or I could make the most of this new life I had been given. I determined to continue my fight until every girl can go to school."[91]

Thus the Malala Fund was created, a charity encompassing her goal of giving girls the opportunities they deserve to pursue and achieve a future they desire. Her work in advocacy and raising funds was deservingly noticed, and Malala was awarded the Nobel Peace Prize in December 2014.[92]

Even when the world's challenges and disadvantageous odds seemed stacked on her, Malala overcame the trauma of her childhood and used it to shape who she became rather than giving up to her unfortunate circumstances.

---

90   Ibid.
91   Ibid.
92   Ibid.

CREATING COMMUNITIES FOR THE FUTURE

The act of turning mistreatment into advocacy is extremely challenging. Often, our initial reaction when harsh treatment falls upon us is a wish for the tormentor to get what they deserve. This seemingly instinctual thought of revenge is a natural reaction that makes it hard to oppose. Indeed, we tend to hear the story of how the school ground bully faced difficult treatment themselves that made them want to inflict the same pain on others. While this was the idea I grew up with, I was shocked to learn that this is not always the case. The man who opened my eyes to this possibility was Guillaume McMartin, a heart-centered social entrepreneur dedicated to helping other social entrepreneurs unleash their true potential.

Guillaume founded an organization bringing community among social entrepreneurs to improve their lives, but his own life was not initially filled with the same sense of joy and community. Since childhood, he never seemed to fit in. At school, his perspective of the world, mature mindset, and passion for learning made him a stereotypical nerd and caused him to be bullied for being different from the other boys in school.

Even in his adulthood, Guillaume faced many hardships. "I didn't know what I wanted to do in my life. I knew I wanted to help people, but I didn't know how," he recalled. Guillaume first went to the police academy to pursue a life of action and helping others but transitioned into becoming a firefighter after two years upon realizing that the policing role didn't suit him.

During this time, Guillaume had a nagging thought of wanting to do more, to contribute toward changing the world. His ambitious goals, different character, and habit of always defending the underdog once again made him a target for bullying. Wanting to do more and seeking a place where he could be accepted, Guillaume decided to take a year off to explore new opportunities in university. And it was one business class that changed his life forever.

One day, he attended a lecture on internet businesses and the law associated with them. It was love at first sight. Immediately after the class, he went up to the professor and asked to attend future classes including one on Business Ideation and Creation (the process of getting an idea and making a business out of it). From that one-hour class, Guillaume felt that he'd found his calling. He decided on that day that, "I'm going to be an entrepreneur. That's how I can be a problem-solver for a living for the world."

Being bullied a lot in his past caused Guillaume to be a very shy person. As such, he tried to do things himself as an entrepreneur in the beginning. "I tried to change the world alone for a year or two, but you just can't do it." So, he reached out and connected with other social entrepreneurs possessing similar passions. It was through his entrepreneurial journey that Guillaume finally found his community.

"I finally felt like there's a place for me to be different and a visionary," Guillaume recalled with a grateful look. "And I realized, there's so much power in a community. We have to get together as social entrepreneurs. Because your strengths are my weaknesses and vice versa. And this is how we can help each other and empower each other to make a big difference."

As Guillaume connected with many people and amazing social entrepreneurs, he came to realize that there are many people around the world, not all exclusively entrepreneurs, with a calling to make a big difference for humanity. It was with this understanding that he created his organization Globalpreneurs, a hub for purpose-driven entrepreneurs to find masterminding, business consulting, and development services to grow themselves and create a sustainable impact.

"We need a community, we need a platform where we can collaborate, share our projects, our ideas, and stop the competition that has been like going on for hundreds of years. It's time for humanity to collaborate because we will just accelerate innovation and progress so much by collaborating and helping each other rather than stepping on each other's toes."

Globalpreneurs was born out of a desire to not let other people feel like they're trying to change the world alone.

Guillaume summarizes the fundamental goal for himself and his organization using the "acorn analogy": He sees social entrepreneurs as an acorn. If you care for that seed you've planted, it's going to grow into a magnificent oak tree. That oak tree is going to produce more acorns that are going to grow for us. "For me, that's what Globalpreneurs is about. Helping one entrepreneur make a difference that's going to empower so many others."

To me, this is a perfect explanation of the ripple effect of impact. When you make a difference on someone, it doesn't just end there. Once you change someone's life, they are empowered and gain self-confidence to impact others in their network, which results in generations of influence, impact, and growth.

Guillaume now embraces his forward-thinking vision and innovative ideas. Despite the difficulties of his past, Guillaume came out positive and inspiring in the end. He did not become a victim of his circumstances. Rather than wallowing in self-pity or cursing the unfairness of his treatment, he was able to overcome them and continue his passion for wanting to help others. Rather than wanting to inflict one's hardships unto others, the single choice of not wanting others to suffer the same way can lead you down a path of impact and positive change.

TAKEAWAYS

While the specifics in all these stories vary greatly, they are united by the common theme of overcoming one's hardships and using it as a push-off point to take control of your destiny.

In each instance and story, the obstacle was by no means easy; the circumstances each character had to overcome were steep, and at first glance, many may not have been most people's first choice. Yet it is only in opposing an unproductive solution and focusing on impact that true change, both from outside and within, can be achieved.

CHAPTER 4

PURPOSE OVER PROFIT

———

In traditional assumptions about economic theory, people lean toward the choice that will make them financially better off. Of course, this belief is not unfounded. Considering that we are each living our own lives, wouldn't it be logical to want to maximize our profit and gain?

My desire to work for a social enterprise—an organization whose primary goal is to work toward a social good—rather than a conventional business focused on profit maximization is motivated by wanting to contribute to something greater than myself. In fact, I was presented with a situation where I had to make this very decision during the Great Quarantine of 2020.

When the COVID-19 pandemic was at its most disruptive stage, I tried to make the most of my quarantine by networking on online platforms. Through making these new connections, I had the honor of receiving two internship positions: the first as the marketing intern for a for-profit social enterprise dedicated to ending hunger in North America, and the other as a business development intern for a business networking organization. As I was seeking to pursue business as a future career path, both experiences offered valuable growth opportunities.

As the marketing intern, my eyes opened to a whole new world of meaningful content and creativity. Tasked with spearheading the organization's Instagram account, I produced creative material using platforms like Canva, which helped to hone my creativity and design skills. As the business development intern, I learned technical skills that I would need to succeed in the business environment, such as sales, CRM management, and entrepreneurship tips.

However, beyond distinct differences in the skills that I learned from these two internships, there was a big difference in financial compensation. As the marketing intern, I had many perks, but no weekly pay. On the other hand, the business development internship offered a commission incentive and weekly bonus.

Managing two internships, writing a book, and doing numerous other impact projects on the side soon took its toll. I came to a point where I realized I had too much on my plate, and to ensure that I could deliver quality work, one of them had to go.

This led to one of the hardest decisions I've had to make. As someone who loves to get involved with all the opportunities around me, this dilemma sparked a brutal internal debate about which internship I had to drop.

During my deliberations, since I believed that the skill development opportunities that each internship offered were equally valuable, the financial aspect and personal satisfaction became the deciding factors. Since I was entering university in the fall, money was attractive. In the end, as I continued to reflect on my enjoyment and experience in these two positions, I realized that my heart had already made the decision.

Something within me yearned to stay with the social enterprise as it was brimming with growth and potential. At the time, the organization had partnered with an interview show, and in each weekly episode, they would talk about the unique "win-win" model that the social enterprise was offering. The value proposition involved ensuring that every contributor who bought food from the company to be distributed to food banks would receive access to a discount app that would allow them to save many times the amount that they gave. Knowing this model, each time the host would make the same rhetorical remark: "Why would you not want to participate in something like this?"

That resonated with me unlike any other. I wanted to support the social enterprise's cause. I realized that the satisfaction of knowing that my contributions would be beneficial for both growing myself and feeding others was more important than monetary value. I believed that the impact I would create was worth more than a paycheck could offer.

So I decided to stay as the marketing intern. While I gained a wealth of knowledge in both my internships, I credit that desire of wanting to make an impact as what helped me make my final choice. Just waking up every day and being able to know that you're working toward something greater than yourself, that you're making a difference in the world, was something that motivated me beyond any other.

Having worked for the social enterprise over the summer, I found myself growing daily. Not only was the work fun in being able to customize posts and engage with different non-profit organizations on social media, but my role also helped me make discoveries. Specifically, I was able to discover just how many purpose-oriented Instagram accounts are on the platform, all offering opportunities to learn, advocate, and get involved with social impact. By exploring this social purpose community, I was able to view the platform as more than a place to waste time scrolling through food pictures and memes. I came to appreciate its value as a platform to create and inspire positive change.

While my personal experience speaks to my choice of choosing purpose over profit, critics who subscribe to the traditional economic theory would argue that outliers may occur when the profit incentive is not great enough. After all, who could truly say that they would turn down a suitcase filled with $1 million for an intangible notion called "purpose"?

However, research is on our side, showing that the correlation between money and happiness is less strong than we think. According to a study by the Gates Foundation, many of the ultrarich are burdened by their wealth and face many anxieties stemming from their fortunes. According to one respondent out of one hundred twenty surveyed people with a net worth of over $25 million, "If we can get people just a little bit more informed, so they know that getting the $20 million or $200 million won't necessarily bring them all that they'd hoped for, then maybe they'd concentrate instead on things that would make the world a better place and could help to make them truly happy."[93]

As the study portrayed, while it is the common assumption to assume that people desire a lavish lifestyle, we are presented with evidence that even the richest people can be left feeling empty or unfulfilled. So what is causing this misalignment with the traditional economic assumption? Is this just the demonstration of a few outliers or is there something more? What prevails in the choice between purpose and profit?

WATERING THE SEEDS OF CHANGE

One of the most respectable stories of purpose and redemption is told through the experience of Scott Harrison, founder and CEO of Charity: Water, one of the world's largest nonprofits dedicated to bringing clean water to everyone on Earth. Yet Scott was not always known for his current life of service. Just a decade ago, he was quite literally "living the dream" of the lavish American lifestyle.

So what moves someone to decide to go from a six-figure income and a hedonistic lifestyle to being the founder of a nonprofit organization? According to Scott's story, the importance of purpose and transformative power of charity can lead one down the path of redemption.

---

93 Robert Frank, "Don't Envy the Super-Rich, They Are Miserable," *The Wall Street Journal*, March 9, 2011.

In 1975, Scott Harrison was born in Philadelphia to a humble life in a Christian middle-class family. Scott grew up in suburbia, and his family moved to a new house soon after his birth to be closer to his dad's job.[94]

On New Year's Day of 1980, Scott's childhood changed forever when his mom collapsed on the bedroom floor. They discovered that this new house had been leaking carbon monoxide from the furnace, which they were not aware of until then. While he and his father got off with no major compromises, the carbon monoxide infected his mother's bloodstream with carboxyhemoglobin, effectively making her allergic to everything. "The toxic gas destroyed her immune system, and in a way, my childhood too," Scott recalled.[95]

Their roles became reversed; to take care of his sick mother, Scott learned to cook and take care of the house. "I was a good Christian kid who played piano in church and wanted to be a doctor when I grew up to help sick people like her." Even into his late teens, Scott never swore, drank, or smoked. Yet that all changed once he turned eighteen.[96]

As music had always been his escape, Scott joined a band and moved to New York in search of the "rock-and-roll game" to make it big. While the band broke up soon after, his experience in producing live music shows introduced him to the prospect of becoming a nightclub promoter where you

94 *INBOUND*, "Scott Harrison | INBOUND 2018 Spotlight," Sept. 7, 2018, video, 1:11:50.

95 *Charitywater*, "The Spring—The charity: water story," Feb. 13, 2020, video, 19:42.

96 INBOUND, "Scott Harrison," 1:11:50.

essentially got paid in the city to drink alcohol for free. Your job? To get people into clubs and charge them hundreds for a bottle of champagne that cost you ten.[97]

Left to his own devices in this concrete jungle of lavish lifestyles, Scott became enamored by the new world around him that he'd been deprived of for so long. Like a child who'd discovered candy for the first time, for nearly a decade Scott gorged himself on many vices; he smoked two packs of cigarettes a day, was drunk almost every night, and had severe drug and gambling problems.[98]

But despite living a life of material contentment, Scott felt unfulfilled. On one New Year's Eve, Scott attended a party in Uruguay which would have looked to outsiders as a "heck of a time." At that place, however, Scott realized how unhealthy and empty his life was.[99]

"I was spiritually bankrupt, I was emotionally bankrupt, I was certainly morally bankrupt. I tried to find my way back to a very lost faith. I wanted things to be different."

Determined on this path of redemption, Scott left the nightlife, sold nearly everything he owned, and made the profound decision of taking a year off to try serving others instead of himself.[100]

---

97 Charitywater, "The Spring," 19:42.

98 Ibid.

99 Ibid.

100 Ibid.

To do that, he set out applying and filling out applications to credible humanitarian organizations. Of course, it turned out to be no surprise when he was denied by them all. His past barred him from even the most basic activity of volunteering. "The organizations were like 'what do you do again? We're serious people.'" Scott described with a chuckle. But he managed to catch a lucky break when an organization told him, "If you pay us $500 a month, you can volunteer with us." Without missing a beat, Scott pulled out his credit card and asked, "Where are you guys going?"[101]

This organization was made up of doctors and surgeons traveling the world on a hospital ship. Specializing in removing facial tumors, the team went to Liberia, one of the poorest countries in the world and one that was entirely unknown to Scott at the time. Using the degree he got from NYU, Scott became the volunteer photojournalist to document the experience and tell the story.

> "Everything in my life changed. I decided in one fell swoop to never smoke again, to never touch drugs again, to never gamble again. I needed to walk so far in the other direction. And I walked up this gangway, and this became my new home."[102]

While he was documenting these life-changing surgeries, Scott spent time in rural villages and witnessed people drinking water that had bugs crawling around in it. Through research, Scott realized that this was the root of numerous

---

101 Ibid.

102 Ibid.

issues that the community was facing. Dirty water causes countless diseases, serving as a greater cause of death than all forms of violence. Approximately 785 million people on Earth don't have access to clean water, and girls forced to sacrifice their education to retrieve water for their families were unjustly rewarded with a disease-carrying water source. People were lacking a basic necessity for survival, and for Scott, this was a problem he could not ignore.[103]

Two years later, Scott returned to New York from the mission fueled by a newfound mission: to bring clean water to everyone on Earth. And interestingly, it began with a party. After getting someone to donate a club, he hosted his thirty-first birthday party where he invited seven hundred people and charged them $20 each. This time, Scott took the money directly to a refugee camp in northern Uganda. The money helped to build three wells, and Scott sent the story back to the donors. "People could not believe that a charity would bother to report to them on a $20 gift, and that something actually happened with the money," Scott explained. And it was with seven hundred people and some $20 donations that Charity: Water was born.[104]

In the process of setting up his charity, Scott found that 42 percent of people in America alone don't trust charities. So he decided to do things differently. Charity: Water differentiated itself in three ways: first, they opened a separate bank account for overhead to ensure that 100 percent of all donations would go directly to clean water. Second, they showed the tangible

---

103 Ibid.
104 Ibid.

impact they were creating by distributing photos and GPS coordinates on Google Maps for people to follow them. Third, they had the work led by locals of the community to ensure future sustainability even after they completed the projects.[105]

Charity: Water built outdoor exhibitions, staged water walks, and designed ads to make people think differently about water. "People started to take notice, and thousands began to donate," Scott remarked proudly. To everyone's pleasant surprise, a movement developed to donate one's birthdays toward clean water.[106]

During one of Scott's speeches, he helped inspire a young girl named Rachel who decided that she wanted to raise $300 for her ninth birthday. She raised $220 and wasn't able to reach her goal, but her parents reassured her that she could try again next year.

She never got that chance. Rachel tragically passed away in a traffic accident. Her legacy, however, lived on. After her death, people began to donate on her fundraising page by the thousands. In just a few weeks, her campaign raised over $1.2 million for clean water.[107]

Rachel's story inspired thousands and helped the movement reach a whole new level. Eighty thousand people dedicated their birthdays to clean water. As Scott explained, "Guys shaved their beards. Strangers started climbing mountains

---

105 Ibid.

106 Ibid.

107 Ibid.

to raise money for clean water. Walking and biking across countries. Sailing across oceans." Over 1 million people have joined the cause and Charity: Water has been able to fund over fifty thousand water projects.[108]

The spin-off effects and positive impact of clean water were the greatest and most fulfilling domino effect. From the benefit of something as simple as clean taps, moms have time to earn money and do other things. Consider this sentence: Kids can take baths, which translates to better focus in school. Access to this simple staple of life helped redefine communities and change the lives of people for the better.[109]

"In the beginning, there was water. Always changing and bringing new life wherever it goes." In the same way, Scott's journey of impact has helped to bring new life to the over 11 million people to whom his organization helped give water. "It did for me, and so many others in very real ways," he reaffirms. "I believe there are only a few times in each of our lives that we get to witness a truly historic, global moment. And giving water to the entire planet will be one of those moments."[110]

Indeed, Scott's story is quite renowned for good reason. It forces you to reconsider your own life, to evaluate where you are now, and opens the opportunity to take a step back and step onto a whole new path. It gives us hope that even if we feel like we've fallen too far, the very act of thinking of how

---

108 Ibid.

109 Ibid.

110 Ibid.

to change oneself is the first step toward meaningful change. Through the action of one man in choosing purpose over profit, Scott laid the groundwork for his dream of giving clean water to everyone on the planet a reality.

FROM PHENOMENON TO NATURE: RE-IMAGINING PURPOSE OVER PROFIT

In my opinion, *purpose over profit* should no longer be considered a phenomenon. Rather, it is an innate nature that pulls at the best of us. According to an article written by Jeremy Adam Smith, an editor of UC Berkeley's *Greater Good Magazine* and a John S. Knight journalism fellow at Stanford University, goals that relate to purpose are often associated with changing the lives of other people. Smith also notes how certain emotions such as awe, gratitude, and altruism can nurture a sense of purpose. The studies conducted by Dacher Keltner of the Greater Good Science Center found that awe fosters connection and the emotional foundation for purpose. William Damon and Robert Emmons among others found that people who expressed greater gratitude were more motivated to give back to their society and thus likely to "contribute to the world beyond themselves." A study by Daryl Van Tongeren then solidified the relationship between altruism and purpose, where people who tended to participate in acts of altruism such as volunteering and philanthropy were more likely to have a greater sense of purpose.[111]

---

111   Jeremy Adam Smith, "How to Find Your Purpose in Life," *Greater Good Magazine,* Jan. 10, 2018.

This research, coupled with Scott's story, presents undeniable evidence of the potential for purpose to take precedent over profit. Further dissenters may argue that Scott's story, like that of Muhammad Yunus, is "one-in-a-hundred." To that end, I am here to provide. Through the following stories of real, average people, I hope to once again prove the power of *purpose over profit*.

FINDINGS FROM THE FENG FAMILY

For six years, my father worked two jobs; he owned a pizza franchise store and worked as a material handler. With both locations in Mississauga, a city over one hundred kilometers away from our home, my dad could only come home once a week and worked the entirety of the remaining six days. While the work was hard, the pay was good, and my family benefited from small luxuries such as annual vacations and new technologies.

In 2016, my dad suddenly announced that he would be selling the pizza store. Of course, this news was delivered much to my mom's chagrin, who enjoyed the extra income that he provided. His decision to work one job came as a surprise to my brother and me as well, but knowing my dad, he wouldn't make decisions without sound logic behind it.

He revealed that as he grew in age, he wanted to spend more time with his family. While his annual earnings took a blow, his action was driven by what he believed to be his most important purpose—of spending time with his family and helping to nurture his children before they went off to university.

In this way, purpose can come in a variety of different forms. Many seem to believe that purpose arises from your special gifts and sets you apart from other people—but that's only part of the truth. It also grows from our connection to others, which is why a crisis of purpose is often a symptom of isolation. Once you find your path, you'll almost certainly find others traveling along with you, hoping to reach the same destination—a community.

Interestingly, gratitude and altruism seem to work together to generate meaning and purpose. In an experiment, the researchers randomly assigned some participants to write letters of gratitude, and those people later reported a stronger sense of purpose. More recent work by Christina Karns and colleagues found that altruism and gratitude are neurologically linked, activating the same reward circuits in the brain.[112]

WORKING FOR PURPOSE: WHAT LIES BEYOND THE WINDOW OF IMPACT

In my view, a lack of purpose can often be easier than it may seem to realize. When you're working at a job for a single and often self-interested purpose, there may arise a smidgen of doubt about the personal satisfaction in your work. I offer the litmus test that if you have to consciously dig through your heart and mind to come up with reasons to justify why you are working somewhere and the value of your work, that

---

112 Christina Karns, "Why a Grateful Brain is a Giving One," *Greater Good Magazine,* Dec. 19, 2017.

unnecessary effort may very well be a red flag for a lacking purpose and an indication for change.

There is something distinctly different about working for purpose, an indescribable bodily experience that I felt myself in the process of conducting my first in-person interview. The next story you will learn about is from Yan Chen, a certified human resources professional specializing in transpersonal psychology in San Francisco. Transpersonal psychology refers to a holistic view of the person and explores the need for meaning inherent within ourselves. As a pioneering learner, she was the first Chinese graduate from the Integral Counseling Psychology program at the California Institute of Integral Studies. Most delightfully, she is the sister of a long-time family friend.

In August of 2020, when my family met with hers for a Chinese get-together celebration, her sister introduced me to Yan as a potential interview prospect as she worked in the social impact space. After learning about this book-writing endeavor that I was undertaking, Yan was immediately interested, and I was of course ecstatic at the opportunity. In hindsight, without this book, I might've never struck up that first conversation with her.

We hit it off immediately as we exchanged thoughts about the future of the social impact space and my aspirations for a purposeful career. As we were at a rowdy dinner party, we arranged for a follow-up one-on-one interview two weeks later. Now, Yan is a free spirit and adventurous by nature, and she was itching to get outside and explore after months of being cooped up at home. So I decided to do something new, to have a trip together to Niagara Falls and conduct an in-person interview there. Yan was ecstatic at the proposition, and the date was set.

The experience I had conducting that in-person interview was unlike any that I'd ever experienced. Deciding to hike along the trails near the falls, we enjoyed a light and engaging conversation while listening to the flow of the water, seeing the life in the forest, and being immersed in the grandeur of nature.

The experience was surreal in how I could practically feel my heart filling as the day went on. It allowed me to realize that what I was doing is important and solidified my goal in writing. If I were to try and describe that feeling, I could only describe it as the feeling of purpose and validation over the value and meaning of my work. Truly, I came to further appreciate the notion of working for purpose, an idea which was further reinforced by Yan's inspiring story.

***

Yan began her career as an operations manager in New York making an above-average salary that allowed her to enjoy a comfortable living. However, everything changed when she had a debate with her boss. Yan is by nature an innovator filled with new ideas, yet her initiative and innovative approach led to a confrontation with her boss in which she was asked, "Who are you? The employee or the company?"

This sat like a rock in her stomach. Yan didn't want to choose. She believed that you shouldn't have to choose between the employee and the company; that we should all be embodying meaning in our work and working toward a shared goal. To Yan, this served as a wake-up call as she was baffled by how her boss was separating these things. "It felt like I was hitting a wall," she explained.

Instead, Yan realized that she wanted to embody meaning in her work. With newfound motivation, she went on to pursue the social impact space, seeking to find a place where she wouldn't be a mere tool for a company, but rather an individual able to express her unique self.

This led Yan to work for numerous international humanitarian organizations like Doctors Without Borders and Refugee International. Her commitment to integrating her experience and passion was inspiring, and she soon became further nurtured by Silicon Valley and the communities there for purpose and innovation. Driven by these prevailing values of fulfillment and innovation, Yan went on to co-found Stage Ai, an education provider offering holistic programs with an emphasis on personal growth, experiential learning, and integral leadership.

She seeks to target adults and youth alike to train them in servant leadership and compassion. Notably, Yan challenges the generational trauma in China that discourages risk-taking. Growing up in that environment herself, she was always told to "be realistic and be safe." However, she has learned through her work in both China and the US that nothing is safe, and entrepreneurship allows you to at least be in control of your own life. By implementing adaptability, creativity, and emotional quotient training into her program,

Yan seeks to disseminate the developmental worldview and foster future leaders that can bring a new movement to her home country.

When asked about how she dared to pursue the social impact space during a time when it was so new, Yan gave the following quote: "It was like I had no choice; once you see a window open to such a beautiful sky of potential, how can you close it and say no?"

TAKEAWAYS

Traditional economic theory is by no means a perfect craft. Indeed, my personal experiences, as well as leading research on philanthropy, have testified to the idea that social purpose and impact can often be a greater incentive than financial prospects. As Scott's story shows, *purpose over profit* is indeed a powerful notion, and even if one has led a self-centered life, it is never too late to change one's ways. For Yan, making the shift into pursuing meaning allowed her to reach a place where she could finally put her passion to action.

With this, the next time that you are faced with a tough decision, look introspectively and consider what is important to you. If you allow purpose to guide you, the destination will always be one filled with fulfillment, passion, and impact.

PART III

IMPACT

CHAPTER 5

COMMUNITY IMPACT

We make a living by what we get, but we make a life by what we give.

—SIR WINSTON CHURCHILL[113]

Foundational to the concept of social impact is the idea of giving. Rooted in the image of altruism and philanthropy, the idea is to give back to the world around us. However, with all the immense issues plaguing our entire world, the needs of those in our own communities can easily be overlooked.

Yet as with the concept of Everyday Impact, every meaningful action starts small, and the experience of working one's way up is truly rewarding. As you will learn from the stories of impact leaders below, social impact is not confined to a macro lens focused on worldwide change; indeed, meaningful change can still be achieved on the community level,

---

113 "We Make a Living by What We Get. We Make a Life by What We Give," Random Acts of Kindness Foundation, accessed Jul. 25, 2020.

and it is in starting small that you can make sustainable, meaningful differences one step at a time.

THE IMPACT BONE

Growing up in a family of immigrants, Dr. Barry Li came to know the importance of giving back from a young age. He found inspiration in his father, who was an active community member and worked to better the lives of others. In tandem, Dr. Li noted with gratitude and nostalgia that he had a lot of people and mentors who helped him when he was growing up to get to where he is now. "I just wanted to give back to the community to the same degree that people have been helping me," he explained. Working hard in his studies, Dr. Li attended the University of Toronto, where he pursued his bachelor's degree in human biology, chemistry, and environmental science.

Since Dr. Li was a child, he had always wanted to become a health-care professional but was never sure which extension of health care that he wanted to pursue. While he explored numerous different extensions of health care at the University of Toronto (UofT) through shadowing programs and extracurriculars, none matched what he was looking for in terms of personal lifestyle and impact.

Things started to get difficult for Dr. Li as his academic responsibilities got harder and he still had no idea what he wanted to do for his career. But it was through his friend (and now wife) Dr. Wang that he was introduced to UofT's External Shadowing Program. By chance, Dr. Li was paired with a chiropractor by the name of Dr. Weisberg, and it set him down a path of passion and service.

During his time in the chiropractic office, what resonated with him most about the career was its flexibility. Rather than sitting in an office-like setting, he was able to be on his feet and interact with patients, allowing him to easily see the change he could make on someone with a job well done.

"To make other people happy, that translates into my own happiness as well. Chiropractic allowed that route," he recalls. "And that is why I decided to do it because I just want to help people and make them happy. That makes me happy, and I want to do things that make me happy for the rest of my life."

Dr. Li went to chiropractic school and had many inspirational experiences. Most notably, his dedication to service led him on five different mission trips to countries such as China and El Salvador, where chiropractic services were not as successful as they were in Canada. Dr. Li particularly recalls a mission trip called the Little Spine, where he provided chiropractic care to six thousand children in Shanghai. In helping to deliver free medical services for those in need, he was able to cultivate his skills while helping people change their health perspective and elevate their life, not just to deliver physical relief. Helping those less fortunate allowed him to foster his heart to serve and validate his goal. "The experience helped me a lot in terms of understanding why I do what I do and my purpose," he remarked with fondness.

Outside of mission trips and volunteering, Dr. Li recalls his life-changing experience in the chiropractic clinic. In 2018,

Dr. Li had just started his training in his school's intern clinic when one day a lady rushed through the door, urgently asking for a chiropractor. Typically, in that kind of case, the clinic will give the client to a senior intern. On this Tuesday afternoon, however, there was nobody else except Dr. Li. His mentor told him, "You know what Barry, there's no one else, so go ahead and take care of this patient." For anonymity reasons, he called this patient Laura.

Laura had acute neck pain, describing it as worse than giving birth. She had fallen asleep on a neck massager which was only meant to be on for ten minutes, so when she woke up in the morning, she could barely move. When Dr. Li asked her about how this pain was impacting her life, Laura told him that she came to the clinic not just because it got in the way of her work as a bartender, but also because her neck was preventing her from interacting with her son and going out to restaurants to buy his favorite rack of ribs. As a mother, she confided in him that she simply couldn't stand that. She wanted to be able to see her family and bring her son's favorite dish.

According to the Hospital for Special Surgery (HSS), acute or chronic pain symptoms can dramatically shift roles and patterns in a family. For example, a parent might not be able to fulfil certain tasks anymore and communication between family members may change based on not wanting to "bother" the affected member.[114] Clearly, Laura was suffering from the consequences of her physical pain which

---

114 Hospital for Special Surgery, "Living with Chronic Pain," *Scleroderma, Vasculitis & Myositis eNewsletter*, Sept. 15, 2013. https://www.hss.edu/conditions_living-with-chronic-pain.asp.

had begun to bleed into her social and family life. "Let's get you better," was what Dr. Li reassured, sympathetic to her plight and determined to help.

In the beginning, Laura was very skeptical as she was not familiar with how effective chiropractic treatment would be. After Dr. Li gave her the first adjustments, just one adjustment to a specific bone in her neck, it released such a huge crack that it seemed to resound throughout the clinic and got Laura to release a sigh of relief and exclaim that it was just what she needed. Dr. Li then told her to go home and rest and arranged to see her again tomorrow.

When Laura came in the second day, she looked like a changed woman. As she walked into the office, Dr. Li noticed that she had done her hair and her make-up, and dressed up in clothing that made her look more put-together than the previous day. It was really interesting to Dr. Li to see this change because it validated a cruel reality of the effects of pain; when people come with acute pain, they don't usually care about anything else since they're distracted by the pain, often even wearing their PJs. "Everything would just really be out of place," Dr. Li explained. So to see Laura's transformation in only one day was extremely satisfying and gratifying for him.

When Dr. Li asked her how she was doing, Laura responded that the adjustment reduced her pain from a 20/10 to an 8/10 from the first visit. She was able to get her son the ribs and have dinner with him that night. But since adjustment doesn't fix everything, they maintained her care for the next two weeks and got her pain down to a 1/10. Further, Dr. Li gave her a plan for the next three months to help her body heal and maintain the progress that she had already made.

As a chiropractor, Dr. Li doesn't just give two to three recommendations. He gives guidelines for lifestyle changes. Rather than putting a Band-Aid on a wound that just keeps on bleeding, he's $100,000 finding the root of the problem like an infection. In doing so, Laura was able to go back to her job and spend time with her family.

Laura saw a full recovery and became an active community member again. Surprisingly, she was a big organizer of the local business networking events in his city and invited Dr. Li as a free guest, which allowed him to talk to many local owners in California. Some of these new connections became patients themselves. Effectively, Dr. Li produced a domino effect that allowed Laura to impact others through his efforts.

A chiropractor's work extends beyond providing relief from physical pain as they can help to change people's lives on a more personal level. By providing the services that allow people to overcome their pain and live a healthy life, these people can in turn better work for their communities and return to being active community members. In doing so, they can impact others in their own way, and foster a cycle of impact.

Currently, Dr. Li continues to bring his passion for the betterment of his community into his work. He goes above-and-beyond; rather than only sticking solely with the roles of a chiropractor, Dr. Li considers himself a passionate community server.

"As a doctor, the most important thing is for us is to connect with the community to impact the community. To understand their needs and make a recommendation based on their needs. In other words, to meet where they're at."

Dr. Li shows a prime example of this concept of *Community Impact*, where you are actively seeking to make a difference in your own backyard. As a chiropractor, he reiterates why he goes above-and-beyond in targeting lifestyle changes: "We do it because we understand that health is so much beyond the condition. It's more about people's lives." In a career, you are not just working for yourself; you are a part of a whole, a gear in the vast machinery that makes up the working function of our societies. Working in the service industry, Dr. Li serves people, and that is his fundamental goal.

"I think the same with any health-care professional. It doesn't matter if you are the world's most accredited. In the end, we're serving people. That's the bottom line."

COMMUNITY IMPACT ON A PERSONAL SCALE

In the Ontario high school curriculum, forty hours of community service is a requirement to graduate from high school. While this is undoubtedly a step in the right direction, I believe that we lack awareness about the actual value of community service.

Not only is community service something we associate with "doing the right thing," it presents several benefits to the volunteer. According to Florida National University, these benefits can be explained using three main buckets:[115]

- Psychological benefits, where volunteers see an increase in overall life satisfaction as the self-fulfillment from helping others improves one's mental state, fighting against stress and depression.

- Social benefits, where volunteers can create unique and valuable relationships with community members. It fosters a sense of social awareness and responsibility.

- Cognitive benefits, where volunteers can grow through real-world, hands-on experience, enhancing their interpersonal skills, such as communication and problem-solving.

Above all, community service should not be seen as something on the checklist of being a "good citizen," but rather a responsibility of giving back to the community in which you live.

With over four hundred hours of community service, I can personally speak to the value of working for others. Subsequently, volunteering has also helped me shape my perspective of the people in my community. A notable example is when I volunteered as a pianist for my local soup kitchen in

---

115 Florida National University Admin, "Why is Community Service Important?" *Florida National University News*, April 8, 2013.

grade twelve, a seemingly simple act that had a profound impact on myself and others alike.

The people who frequented the soup kitchen were those that society often tends to dismiss owing to the negative stereotypes that project a less-than-ideal image of danger or pity. Volunteering for the soup kitchen, however, was a humbling experience as it completely shattered those preconceived notions. I came to develop relationships with a group of wholesome people unique in their own right. These were not the shells of people that the media depict them to be; these were individuals with astounding talents and stories that I hadn't appreciated enough before.

During the cold November evenings when I would play the piano during the dinner service, I filled the lobby with classical music as people filed in. As people got in line, ate, and left, I would often receive compliments on my playing and comments of gratitude for the way that my music gave the place a livelier tone and a sense of home.

Nearly every time I went, there would be someone who would always stand beside the piano and watch me play. He told me how he was a musician himself, and when he asked if he could play a song, I moved over. What came next completely blew me away. He began to play Claire de Lune entirely by ear with a perfect melody and rhythm. Indeed, the people I met at the soup kitchen were unlike any I'd ever expected to meet. Through this seemingly simple volunteering experience, I was able to grow on a personal level while bringing joy to the community.

I may not have been exposed to as many real work experiences as adults. However, my greatest growth experiences have come from community service. Starting with helping our communities is one of the best ways to make a positive impact and make lasting memories. There are so many benefits to be had, so make the most of them, leverage your experiences, and commit to them with a genuine passion and kindred spirit.

IMPACT WITHIN ONE'S OWN BACKYARD

When we think about social impact, our mind conjures images of impoverished lands in developing countries. Mission trips can indeed be meaningful, but social impact isn't restricted to those endeavors; often, the most realistic and effective means of making a difference can present itself in your very community.

I came to understand the potential in community impact firsthand while working with OneChild, an NGO advocating against child sex trafficking. While the crime is especially prevalent in vulnerable developing countries, working with OneChild as their research assistant was eye-opening. As I worked with the then executive director of the organization, she relayed anecdotes of this terrible crime occurring right where I lived. As I conducted more research about the facts of child sex trafficking in Canada, I was completely floored.

Human trafficking in Canada reached a peak of three hundred forty incidents in 2016, an increase of more than 600 percent since its first recorded statistic in 2009. Of the eight hundred sixty-five total victims of human trafficking that were identified between 2009 and 2016, ninety-five percent of them were women, seventy-two percent were under the age of twenty-five, and over a fourth were under the age of eighteen.[116]

These facts terrified me. Beyond that, they angered me. I became frustrated not only at the cruelty of the crime but also at my own inertia in tackling this terrible issue that's happening right under my nose.

I threw myself into research for OneChild to create a social return on investment (SROI) report that would help to rally donors toward the cause of child sex trafficking prevention. I embraced an unconventional approach: To determine the costs of trafficking, I put myself in the victim's shoes. I pictured rough hands gripping my hair, purple blooming across my skin, the mental anguish of someone whom I thought loved me becoming my tormentor. I then found resources that would provide me with a dollar value to the health, legal, and rehabilitation services that I would need after that hell. When I noticed that online resources were insufficient, I overcame my timidity to contact the Department of Justice and over twenty organizations myself to gather data.

After three hundred and twenty-five hours of number-crunching and writing, I created the first ever SROI report identifying the cost of child sex trafficking on the Canadian economy. With the printed paper in hand, I relished in the knowledge that my work would promote the value of funding prevention

---

116 "Trafficking in Persons in Canada, 2016," statcan.gc, accessed July 23, 2020, https://www150.statcan.gc.ca/n1/pub/85-005-x/2018001/article/54979-eng.htm.

to prevent future children a lifetime of suffering. I was overcome by that indescribable yet distinct euphoria of finding your *joie de vivre* (happiness in life).

My community impact experience of working with OneChild made me aware of the fact that many social issues such as child sex trafficking do not discriminate: they can affect anyone. This idea is not specific to child sex trafficking either. Every country struggles with crime and socioeconomic difficulties in certain areas. What does it say about us if we can't even contribute toward the issues happening in our communities?

It was the end of my co-op, yet this discovery of my altruistic passion began my journey of impact. I continued working with OneChild as a student representative where I contacted local organizations to help OneChild secure speaking opportunities, all to educate others about how we can prevent the occurrence of this crime in our community.

Moving forward, I planned service projects in Key Club to make a difference in my community. When volunteering as the pianist for my local dementia ward and soup kitchen, I played the piano like I typed my SROI report: with a mind dedicated to the goal of positive impact and a heart swelling with the satisfaction of doing good for others. In my four hundred hours of community service, I became aware of the power and presence of my altruistic motivation.

As I mentioned before, there is so much to gain from going. Beyond the self-induced benefits from fulfilment, creating value for your community can allow you to gain even greater returns through community support. For a community leader like Rosa Lokaisingh, her story encompasses this very advantage.

THE VALUE OF HEART-CENTERED BUSINESS

"It takes a village to bring up a child, but it takes a community to grow a business."

Such is Rosa's community-oriented philosophy to business. Rosa Lokaisingh is an entrepreneur, business coach, and master networker who embodies the idea of heart-centered business.

While she's enjoyed a life of success in the corporate world, Rosa has committed the majority of her life to community service. Growing up, Rosa found her primary inspiration from her father, a schoolteacher who made great strides within his community. When Rosa was nine and living in Trinidad, her father received a position with the government called the community social aid and threw himself into the community. "Just traveling with him and seeing the impact that he had on the very community that we lived in inspired me so much. I saw the joy in his eyes when he was serving."

Rosa recalled her childhood with a fond tone. "It was just like a permanent smile in my heart, being with him and watching what he did. And I resonated with it. Somehow it just stuck with me, because as I grew up, I saw myself doing the same thing." In her teenage years, Rosa always found a way to involve herself with the community by volunteering at senior homes and donating toys to the Children's Hospital.

Much of her passion for service also came from an innate awareness. Since she was young, Rosa was conscious of social issues such as world hunger. "I couldn't understand it. I knew it was unjust and unfair. I didn't have the solution, but I wanted to find a solution." From this sense of wanting to make a difference, Rosa was drawn to leadership to obtain the power and influence to make a difference.

When Rosa grew older and started working, she was offered leadership positions. But as time went on, she noted a fundamental flaw with the way certain businesses treated staff. "How could you ask your staff to come into work, enthusiastic and motivated when you are not providing any resources, comfort, or appreciation for them to show up that way?" she questioned.

From her position, Rosa knew that change was not going to happen promptly in large corporations. To make a difference, Rosa vowed to create her own change: That when she had her own business, she would do what these large businesses failed to do. "Small entrepreneurs have more capacity to make changes because they're the decision-makers," Rosa explained. Soon after, she quit her banking job and started her own business.

In the process of developing her business, Rosa would reflect on the difference it would make if the world of business worked with open hearts. In other words, what impact would kindness in the workplace have? To this end, Rosa determined that not only would it increase morale, but the positivity could follow workers to their own homes and feed that forward to their family. In essence, it shows the impactful ripple effect of positivity, and once again shows how small actions can grow and can become even bigger than we may initially perceive them to be.

What made Rosa stand out was her commitment to her fundamental values of service and giving. When Rosa came to Canada from Trinidad, she continued her entrepreneurial goals. Despite the immense time and stress it must have taken to build one's way up in a new society, Rosa quickly established herself through community service. She got together with many community members to clean up the Don Valley river in her city of North York, receiving an award for her efforts from the mayor. She volunteered with the women's shelter, raising over $500 by hosting a Caribbean New Year's Eve party that brought people together. Impacting people of all ages, Rosa worked with kids in the neighborhood of Regent Park in Toronto, where she would help them create vision boards, identify their goals, and create action plans for their future.

Throughout her professional career, she has never lost sight of her community values. Even during the COVID pandemic, after seeing that people were hurting and feeling isolated, Rosa thought to host online mastermind groups to help people connect. Inspired by a coach of hers in California, she started a formal online gathering event, which she called the "Town Hall Gathering of Hearts and Minds." Seeing the various challenges that people were trying to fix alone, she offered a platform for them to come together and help each other brainstorm.

Participants provided Rosa with glowing praise, stating that they felt safe in the trusting environment where they could open their hearts without feeling too vulnerable. They became comfortable sharing not just their ideas, but also their emotions, helping each other come up with ideas for pivoting their business through COVID.

I have had the pleasure of attending a few of Rosa's Town Hall gatherings myself. It's something about the way she attracts people who are also heart-centered, like the law of attraction. Her extensive experience in serving others and helping her community grew within her an aura that just made you feel comfortable with her.

As we reached the end of our interview, Rosa provided a final comment about the importance of community in business. "It takes a community to grow a business." She declared. As a business coach, Rosa saw many of her clients go on to become very successful because they chose to do a heart-centered career that engaged their passion and allowed them to prac-tice service.

Rosa's signature motto is "My life is my passion." In this vein, she recommends that everyone behave in a genuine way to bring purpose to their careers. In both business and daily life, Rosa advises listening to people with an open heart to make a genuine connection with them. "When you make one connection to the heart of another human being, you can have that connection for life." These connections would result in mutual benefits, with support coming in a two-way street. And to build a connected world, for global impact, we must start one community at a time.

COMMUNITY SHAPING IMPACT, IMPACT SHAPING CAREER

This final example follows a community leader named Efosa Obano, the founder of the African Impact Initiative, an organization offering professional development and community building for African students in Africa and Canada.[117] For Efosa, a sense of community has always been one of his greatest values, especially stemming from his university experience. Effectively, his journey shows how it is in understanding your community's needs, responding to those needs, and interacting with them that you can position yourself in a way that will best suit you and those around you.

Efosa grew up in Nigeria and moved to Canada in search of greater educational opportunities. At the time, his country was also facing security issues, militant groups, and violence, but he was lucky that his parents could afford to send him to Canada for his university education. Beginning his study at the University of Toronto, he essentially had to rebuild an entire life from scratch.

Being an introvert in a new country made his first year extremely challenging. Similar to the "new kid in school" situation, he struggled to fit in with the university environment.

---

117 "Impacting Africa Through Our Youth," African Impact Initiative, accessed July 23, 2020.

While Efosa was gradually able to connect with a few people in the African community, he described feeling a sense of imposter syndrome as it seemed that everyone had a friend from their high school in his program. Over time, Efosa was able to make friends along the way through arduous efforts and dedication. He put in great efforts to prove to others his worth in classroom contributions and went out of his way to engage with peers. During his second year, he built a community for himself

He quickly came to embrace the diversity on campus, and from personal experience, became driven by the motivation to work so that no other students would face the same struggles that he went through. So he decided to work on improving the student experience for other African immigrants.

In his second year, Efosa founded the African Students Association (ASA), an organization providing social and cultural events to bring UofT's African students together. As their events went on, Efosa learned extensively from this new community he'd cultivated. "We would find ourselves often speaking about how bad things were for where we call home, and how much we wanted to change that through what we're learning with our degrees," he explained. "We also talked about how hard it was for African immigrants settling into the system just like ourselves when you come here in terms of getting jobs and careers."

Efosa noted how age and experience became an obstructive factor, explaining that he felt like his group had to wait and "grow up" until they could do anything to change the situation. "But there was a kind of like a restlessness in me to get to take action. To do something more." Efosa explained how that planted the seed for what would become the African Impact Initiative.

In the summer of 2016, Efosa sought to bring more comprehensive professional resources to the African community. To advance the opportunities for African youth in Canada, he started on campus by engaging corporations to give specific skill-based training for members to get jobs and boost employability. They hosted LinkedIn workshops and brought in African professionals to offer their perspectives and how they navigated the workforce after graduation.

They began to receive more recognition on campus for their projects, but since Efosa and his co-founder were graduating in 2018, they recruited a new team of students. The founding team, without the burden of school and assignments, decided to dedicate more time to expand the organization, leading to the birth of ASA's second, international-focused chapter.

With his new group, Efosa was inspired and determined to create an impact beyond his university community and in his country from which he came. So began a new chapter as Efosa and his team went back to Southern Nigeria and tried to tackle the challenges in his home country.

Their first project was focused on improving health-care outcomes for the Ikot Eko Ebon rural community. In partnership with Cottage Hospital and the Akwa Ibom government, they were able to increase the number of people in that village who received quality care by revamping their community hospital with equipment to address their pressing health issues.[118]

But during this experience, Efosa realized the challenge of bringing resources back and forth between countries. From this he discovered that pushing a solution from outside is inefficient; what is more effective is a solution from within.

Efosa created the African Impact Challenge to enable sustainable development locally in Africa by investing in youth to solve identified problems through technology driven impact entrepreneurship. Rather than trying to come in as outsiders to fix a problem, Efosa and his team began to sow the seeds of problem-solving and entrepreneurship within the community. This would allow them to bypass the time and resources used in travelling while ensuring that the communities themselves could continue innovating on their own.

In his professional career, working at Bell as their CSR lead, Efosa has seen firsthand the great things that technology can do for the world. By providing communities with the technology and capital necessary to facilitate their own innovative ideas, Efosa hopes to promote a sustainable approach to problem-solving.

"We're looking to solve problems, not necessarily just to have an idea. It needs to be meeting a need in the local community, which the people that want to solve it can identify with."

---

118 *African Impact Initiative,* "African Impact Rural Health Care Project (Shortened Version)," January 30, 2019, Video, 5:07.

Partnering with top universities in Ghana, over the next five years, the program will provide the capital, resources, and mentorship for innovations with a $100,000 CAD fund.[119]

Efosa has carved for himself an incredible story of growth. As noted by Florida National University, for students, community service can be largely beneficial to career prospects by allowing them to obtain work-related skills, professional references, and forums to network with potential employers. Beyond that, it fosters skills in social responsibility and an awareness of community needs. Through it, one may very well develop a passion for life.[120]

Today, Efosa continues to dedicate himself to the social impact sphere and serves as the social impact pillar lead for Dell Canada. From being the "new kid," Efosa worked his way up by creating a community for his peers. This evolved to become an impactful organization benefiting people globally and becoming a fundamental aspect that shaped his career.

TAKEAWAYS

As I explained in my inspiration chapters, our communities can have a significant influence on our identity. In the same way, we can have a great impact on shaping our communities.

Community service should not be seen as a chore done for the sake of getting it done; rather, it is being genuine

---

119 African Impact Initiate, "Impacting Africa Through Our Youth," July 23, 2020.

120 Florida National University, "Why is Community Service Important," April 8, 2013.

in wanting to benefit your community that you will reap the benefits of those experiences. Being conscious of your community needs can not only help you to develop your own leadership capabilities but also allow you to grow your network and reach people through your genuine self.

Everyday Impact can be achieved right in our own communities, and the value of this impact can be many times worth the investment.

CHAPTER 6

POWER OF KINDNESS

———

Treat others the way you want to be treated.

Such was the motto of my elementary school. Nearly a decade later, the message has not been forgotten.

Looking back now, hearing this motto repeated over and over during the formative years of my childhood made a big difference. My obedient and eager-to-please eight-year-old self took this to heart, with an internal dialogue that probably went something like this: "I want to be treated kindly and with respect, so I guess that means I have to do the same for everyone else too!"

It quickly became a habit, an easy behavior to uphold. I remember thanking my teachers after each class, feeling a comforting warmth spread through me when they returned a soft smile. I would stay after school to sweep the floor of my portable classroom after my classmates spread dirt all over it. I would never badmouth anyone, refusing to be insulting behind others' backs and rather wanting to support my peers whenever I could.

Seeing the smiles from my small acts made me feel warm and giddy inside, but I never thought anything more of it. I don't think I ever fully knew or appreciated the impact of kindness until now—until I'd received it myself from others who've supported me in my book. And truly, it has only further enlightened me on the power of kindness in making a meaningful difference.

BUILDING OURSELVES ON KINDNESS

This book is built on kindness.

As a testament to my claims of how small actions can make a big impact, throughout my book-writing journey, I have been so positively impacted by the support and kind actions of the incredible people I've met. Among those are the professionals who kindly accepted to interview with me to share their story. Others include those who reached out to me themselves to provide their support. In this case, a notable story I hope to share about kindness comes from an incredible individual who reached out to me first; and while she began simply by offering her support, I came out with an inspiring story.

EVERYDAY KINDNESS AND THE SUPERPOWER IN US ALL

During an online masterminding session in mid-July of 2020, I met Brenda Marie Sheldrake, a network and sales expert serving as a licensee of the organization Selling On The Spot Marketplace. As I delivered my elevator pitch for my book during the session, she reached out to me to ask if there was anything that she could do to support me in my authorship journey. Moved, I immediately arranged a call with her.

I didn't have any initial expectations for the call. Brenda wasn't a social impact director or involved with the traditional impact route of nonprofits. As I learned her story, however, I realized that she was exactly the person I was looking for.

Brenda turned out to be one of the most genuine people I've ever met, with a genuine heart to serve.

Brenda worked with Czech families with disabled family members who arrived in Canada as refugees. Many of them have disabilities, and she's been trying to help them get the disability tax credit that can help support them in the new country. She doesn't charge people to do this process, but Brenda noted that the process is very cumbersome due to the language barrier. So what she ended up doing, as she explained, was doing their appointments with their children—of whom were more well-versed in both English and Czech—as the translators.

During this time, she met with many families. But one particularly stood out, as the mother was blinded by an inoperable brain tumor while the father was deaf. So their fifteen-year-old daughter was doing all the translating for her family, setting up health appointments, essentially being the adult because she had to be. "Talk about being robbed of your childhood," Brenda noted sadly.

Brenda wanted to do something to help this little girl, so she decided to pay her like she would a real interpreter during sessions with her mother. Now what's most unique and heart-warming about this exchange is that Brenda didn't pay her in the traditional sense with an hourly wage.

"I gave her a Tim Hortons card. I gave her a Netflix card. I'm going to give her gaming cards so that she can play some games. And hopefully, she can get a little enjoyment, and be a kid for just a little while with the cards that I give her," Brenda explained fondly.

After that appointment, two things happened. The girl was happy to be paid in a meaningful way for her work, and her mother had hope that she would get the money that the government offered. When Brenda walked them to the exit of her building, the mother turned around abruptly. Despite knowing only a few words of English, she said, "thank you so much for helping my family," with all her heart. The woman then declared that she was going to hug Brenda. So with open arms, Brenda welcomed her into a warm hug.

At this time Brenda looked directly at me, her face softening as she explained,

"And for that two minutes she was hugging me, you could forget about COVID. It was just two people just connecting, and I knew I'd made a difference in her life. That hug made more difference in my life than if I'd made $5,000."

Just hearing this, I was left speechless by the sheer impact that such a seemingly simple action would have had. What stands out is how Brenda "tailored" her act of kindness in a way for the little girl. While random acts of kindness can help make our communities better overall, it's important to remember that they shouldn't always be done with a "'one-size-fits-all" sort of attitude. The impact of an act done after taking into account the other's situation and finding the best way to improve their life can be exponentially greater. In taking that extra step, Brenda went above-and-beyond. She augmented her impact, transforming it from a simple act of kindness to a more unique and meaningful action. Even if the act wasn't done for me, it is one that even I wouldn't soon forget.

Finally, Brenda explained how she uses her career as a way to create impact. Brenda is a networker, so when she books a Zoom with someone, she has a conversation with them about two things: your superpower and your kryptonite.

Brenda believes that everyone has a superpower—something that they specialize in, essentially their greatest strength—and asks a series of questions to identify what that superpower is. After recording that superpower in her spreadsheet, she gets the person to identify what they believe their kryptonite to be. "So, what do you think it is, what is that one thing that if you could change it, you think you could be even more powerful and effective," Brenda would ask.

As an example, Brenda conducted her superpower and kryptonite test on me right then during our interview. My superpower, to her, is my ambition, which drives me to do things that others wouldn't normally do to achieve my dreams. My kryptonite, however, is my perfectionism which tends to force me to spend more time on something needlessly in an attempt to strive for an unrealistic standard.

Once she identifies someone's superpower and kryptonite, Brenda points out the fact that "your superpower is someone else's kryptonite." She emphasizes that no matter what your superpower may be, there is someone out there who is looking to learn from someone like you. That there is a person out there who can help you overcome your biggest weakness.

Brenda records these things and keeps a log of the superpowers and kryptonite of the people she speaks with, even if she doesn't formally ask. So with that, Brenda seeks to get people connected both with people they can help through their superpower, as well as people that can help them with their kryptonite. "This is not something I do to make money," Brenda confesses. "This is something I do that fills my cup up. One person at a time, one day at a time, I can make huge differences for hundreds of people."

After speaking with Brenda, not only was I humbled by the way that she exemplifies the power of "Everyday Impact," but I was intrigued by this idea of "kindness as a superpower." I wanted to know if this idea of the impact and superpower-esque ability of kindness could be testified by others.

PERSONAL REFLECTIONS, PROFOUND DISCOVERIES

As I began to reflect on this idea, I realized I'd seen an example of this in my own life.

During the fall of 2017, I'd gotten my first part-time job working at Tim Hortons. With this role in customer service, despite working the morning shift on busy weekends, I would greet customers with an energetic voice and bright attitude. From the simple act of expressing positive energy, customers would thank me for brightening up their day, spreading the welcomed contagion of positivity to start their morning off on a good note.

While I might not have stopped global warming or donated thousands to charity, I still made a small but undeniably positive impact on someone. That person, with a new positive attitude, would be able to pass that positivity to others, thus continuing this domino effect of impact that I started.

What we often overlook or perceive to be too small can surprise us. Through Brenda's story and my reflection, it was inspiring to discover how a little bit of kindness can go a long way. I want to show you just how powerful kindness can be, and how it's the superpower that all of us have.

Recall that social impact is defined by any action that creates a change in the communities around you. In this way, even the simplest of actions, even just bringing a smile to another person's face can make a difference in the community around you. With all these powerful narratives testifying the power of kindness, I sought to validate this power through empirical evidence. Incredibly, not only is the quantity of research conducted humbling, but many testify to the positive benefits that kindness can have on the beholder as well.

Numerous studies have shown that natural altruistic and volunteering behavior are related to physical benefits including lower blood pressure to psychological benefits such as increased life satisfaction and decreased depression.[121]

The incentives of engaging in kind actions speak for themselves as their benefits are backed by research. In a study conducted by Lyubomirsky, Sheldon, and Schkade, 2005 and Lyubomirsky, Tkach, and Sheldon, 2004, when monitored over six weeks, students who performed five acts of kindness one day per week demonstrated significant improvements in well-being compared to the control group.[122]

Seeking to find more expert opinions, the stories detailing the power of kindness are more plentiful and impactful than I ever expected. While they share the common theme of kindness as a superpower, they each present a unique lesson on how it can be leveraged to its fullest potential.

3 INSIGHTS FOR POWERFUL KINDNESS

KINDNESS PAYS OFF

The power of kindness stands as a common theme in TED Talks, the world's most renowned speeches. Carrying the name "Kindness is your superpower," the talk delivered by Marly Q. Casanova epitomizes this very idea.

---

121 Sarah Pressman et al., "It's Good to Do Good and Receive Good: The Impact of a 'Pay It Forward' Style Kindness," *Journal of Positive Psychology* 10, no. 4 (2014): 1-10.

122 Sonja Lyubomirsky et al., "Pursuing Happiness: The Architecture of Sustainable Change," *Review of General Psychology* 9, no. 2 (2005): 111-131.

As a child, Marly always wished for superpowers that could help her save the world. But after being devastated that she couldn't develop supernatural powers to clean up the environment, her teacher told her that "kindness is your superpower." Her teacher explained how the small things she did like pushing in the chairs after class and smiling at others brightened up her day. This inspired Marly like none other. She notes that at ten years old, she became living proof of Aesop's famous quote: "No act of kindness, no matter how small, is ever wasted."[123]

When Marly was in grade nine, she notes how another teacher changed her life by forcing her to run as president for the school's community service club. While she was resistant at first, the push she got from her teacher set off a ripple effect which not only allowed her to be unanimously voted into the role but also helped her graduate with over three thousand hours of community service. Her extensive involvement granted her the ability to attend any school in the nation with a fully paid bachelor's and master's degree.

"I began to realize that being kind pays off. Literally."[124]

As Marly's story shows, kindness can not only lead to positive internal effects. Research from Emory University showed that being kind to another stimulates your brain's pleasure and reward centers in the same way as if you had received that good deed yourself. Nicknamed the "helper's high" from

---

123 *TEDx Talks*, 'Kindness is Your Superpower | Marly Q | TEDxJWUNorth-Miami," Feb 28, 2018, Video, 20:39.

124 Ibid.

psychologists studying generosity, the act of being kind has been theorized to release the same endorphins (the feel-good, warm chemicals) associated with the runner's high.[125] In 2010, Harvard Business School also surveyed happiness in one hundred thirty-six countries with incredible results; the responses showed that altruistic people were happiest overall.[126]

As a York University study found, "there is karma in kindness." The study showed that people who engaged in small acts of kindness for just five to fifteen minutes results in higher happiness and self-esteem levels. According to a co-author of the study, "It is also possible that being kind to others may help us be kind to ourselves," and that can arguably be the greatest payoff.[127]

KINDNESS HAS A PROFOUND RIPPLE EFFECT

A similar story follows in the talk from Orly Wahba titled "The Power of Kindness," where she describes how, since she was four years old, she always wanted to change the world. Despite being labelled an unrealistic "dreamer," she worked hard to turn that dream into reality through the organization she started called "Life Vest Inside." The organization seeks to empower individuals toward their own potential

125 James Boraz and Shoshana Alexander, "The Helper's High," *Greater Good Magazine*, Feb. 1, 2010.

126 Lara B. Aknin et al, "Prosocial Spending and WellBeing: Cross-Cultural Evidence for a Psychological Universal," *American Psychological Association* 104, No. 4, 635-652.

127 Valerie Hauch, "Kindness Pays Off, Study Finds," *Toronto Star*, May 18, 2011.

for impact and unite the world with kindness because while we can't prevent the mishaps, curveballs, and tragedies that come our way, we can throw someone a life vest—a lifeline of kindness—that can help save them.[128]

As a grade-eight teacher, Orly first began to do a bunch of projects with her students that followed this same concept of kindness, like kindness cards. But she took this one step further. "I want to show people the ability that kindness has to go from one person to the next and truly transform them, giving them that sense of meaning and purpose." So with a background in film production and a zillion post-it notes like a scene out of a *Beautiful Mind*, Orly shot *Kindness Boomerang*, a short film that followed the ripple effect of a kind action before boomeranging back to the original giver.[129]

The video achieved an unpredictable reception, reaching over a hundred million people in only a few months. Orly soon started getting messages from all over telling her about how it's changed their life, inspired them, and even saved them from suicide.[130]

One message Orly carries with her is from a man named Frederick. He wrote that he was going through many hardships and experienced no support until he saw one of Orly's posts on Facebook about kindness. It helped him find inner

128 *TEDx Talks,* "The Power of Kindness | Orly Wahba | TEDxStPeterPort," April 1, 2016, Video, 21:31.

129 Ibid.

130 Ibid.

peace and forgiveness. He wrote to her about how he's now back on track and volunteers for a place for homeless kids.[131]

> "This may not appear like a big deal to you, but you saved a life—you changed someone's life story. You opened the gates to a better future for a human being. You made me happy again and what I learned from you I'm giving to others. You may not have changed the world, but you changed my world."
>
> —FREDERICK[132]

Orly concludes by saying that it's the simple things everyone can do that can make a big difference. "Kindness is such a broad term but when we look at the simple things, suddenly we start to see them popping up everywhere."[133]

The phenomenon that Orly experienced and started regarding the "ripple effect" of kindness is supported by facts itself. As noted by the Random Acts of Kindness organization, not only will you and the receiver benefit from the kind act, but it can also go on to impact third parties and anyone who witnesses the act as they will often be inspired to "pay it

---

131   Ibid.

132   Ibid.

133   Ibid.

forward."[134] Noted in the "Kindness Contagion" by assistant professor of psychology at Stanford University Jamil Zaki, a single good deed done in a crowded area can inspire a domino effect among witnesses to do the same, thereby improving the lives of dozens of people.[135]

James Fowler, the professor of medical genetics and political science at the University of California, also found in one of his studies this very same "pay-it-forward" phenomenon, as a single kind act would often inspire several other acts of generosity. Known formally as "upstream reciprocity," this chain of altruism is truly a "domino effect of warm and fuzzy feelings."[136]

KINDNESS CHANGES LIVES

This recurring message of kindness having the ability to change lives is intimately expressed by TED speaker Jenny Schell in her talk "Everyday Kindness and Simple Giving Matter."[137]

"We make a living by what we get. We make a life by what we give." This was how Jenny Schell, CEO of the creative design firm Design Rangers, started off her TEDxColoradoSprings

134 "Kindness Health Facts," Random Acts of Kindness, accessed Jul. 16, 2020.

135 Jamil Zaki, "Kindness Contagion," *Scientific American*, July 26, 2016.

136 Jessica Cassity, "Why One Act of Kindness is Usually Followed by Another," *Goodnet*, Dec. 24, 2014.

137 *TEDx Talks*, "Why Everyday Kindness and Simple Giving Matter | Jenny Schell | TEDxColoradoSprings," Jan. 5, 2017, Video, 10:35.

speech. As a Colorado Springs native, Jenny has a long and surprising history in the Pikes Peak region.[138]

Jenny is an active community member who has used her skills to create impact: She served as Creative Director of a local philanthropic initiative called Give!, used her designs to create Wild Fire Tees during the Waldo Canyon Fire, and shared her inspiring childhood stories in events such as Walmart's 2016 "Fight Hunger. Spark Change." campaign, raising over $17 million for Feeding America and $107,000 for Care and Share. At the TEDxColoradoSprings event in 2017, Jenny shared her story once more.[139]

"I constantly feel compelled to give, even in just tiny ways that I know will help to brighten someone's day," Jenny remarks. "My therapist tells me it's because I've been there. I know first-hand that everyday kindness and simple giving can change a person's life."[140]

Indeed, Jenny had an unconventional and challenging childhood. After her parents' divorce, her mother took custody of her while seeking to fulfil her dream to live life "off the grid." They moved to Lawrence, Colorado, a late 1800s ghost town, living in a mountain home carrying no running water or electricity. According to Jenny, this "off-the-grid life" taught her "a lot about hard work, simple pleasures, and being resourceful. It was also just as tough and full of struggle as

---

138 Ibid.

139 Ibid.

140 Ibid.

you might imagine. In addition to their precarious living conditions, the family struggled to make ends meet.[141]

"I also learned about food distribution, and that the days we drove to pick up the food stamps were good days. But if they ran out before the end of the month, we knew the grocery store sometimes threw out food. And if we went into their dumpster after they closed, we could typically find enough to make a few simple meals, and maybe even a treat for my cats."[142]

As Jenny recalled with a bittersweet twinge, how did she get from that ghost town to the TEDx stage in Colorado Springs? How did she stay and pursue the positives despite the darkness and negatives? "I'm convinced it's because of the people who reached out and gave without even realizing how important their kindness and simple gifts were to me and my mom," Jenny confessed.[143]

Jenny recalled how their closest neighbors would offer to babysit her at four a.m. so her mom could make it to her restaurant job. The warm sourdough pancakes they made each morning gave her energy and hope. Jenny learned that holding onto the joy despite the hardships of life made life easier and fun.[144]

---

141 Ibid.

142 Ibid.

143 Ibid.

144 Ibid.

"These kind, generous people and so many more taught me that giving, in any form, makes the dark days brighter, and the hopeless days shimmer with hope."[145]

At the end of her moving speech, Jenny asked the audience to do two things: "think back and remember one time when someone's kindness made an impact on your life." She then asked them to consider: "what acts of kindness or small, simple gifts can you act on?" Jenny lists a few small acts of kindness, including a heartfelt card to a coworker going through a tough time, some compassion for an elderly person who is hard-of-hearing and doesn't remember things well, or simply the cliché cup of coffee for the person behind you in line.[146]

Jenny's story sheds light on the true power of small acts of kindness in changing one's life. She acknowledges how our current society makes it easy to get overwhelmed by the thought of giving, faced with the pressure that we need massive amounts of time or money to make a difference. But Jenny concludes that "your kindness makes all the difference in the world, and without even knowing why, or how, it could help to change somebody's life, sending them down a different path than the one that was plotted before you arrived."[147]

Such a lesson is most relevant especially during these times. Kindness, during the darkest times, can stand out like a beacon of light. Particularly during the 2020 pandemic, small acts of kindness were increasingly covered as a little truly

---

145 Ibid.

146 Ibid.

147 Ibid.

went a long way. From giving food to the hungry to creating face masks for frontline workers, the pandemic highlighted how much a small act could influence someone's life. As a particular headline from CBC News summarizes, "Small acts of kindness have big impact amid pandemic."[148]

TAKEAWAYS

Small actions, even if they may at first glance seem insignificant, can make a greater positive impact and difference than we believe. Not only is it a superpower that everyone holds, but in giving to others, you are also receiving and reaping emotional rewards and health benefits.

With the "pay-it-forward" phenomenon, simply witnessing or learning about kindness and generosity can spur one to engage in acts of kindness themselves. I hope that from the stories you've read, you will be inspired to embrace the superpower of kindness within yourself to change your and others' lives for the better.

---

148 Sidney Cohen, "Small Acts of Kindness Have Big Impact in the N.W.T. Amid Pandemic," *CBC News*, April 23, 2020.

CHAPTER 7

EVERYDAY ADVOCACY

When the world is silent, even one voice becomes powerful.
—MALALA YOUSAFZAI[149]

Advocacy, according to the Merriam-Webster dictionary, is defined as "the act or process of supporting a cause or proposal."[150] With the rise of mental health and global issue advocates, the simple act of spreading awareness can be relevant to advocacy.

Yet what does it mean to be an advocate? With just one person and small actions, how can advocacy lead to real change?

These beliefs should sound familiar, as they reflect much of what people also think about social impact as a whole. In the same way that I promote the power of small actions through Everyday Impact, the concept of small actions that compound over time applies in the field of advocacy. In the

---

149 "Malala Yousafzai Quotes," Goodreads, accessed Aug. 27, 2020.

150 *Merriam-Webster*, s.v. "Advocacy," accessed Sept. 5, 2020.

stories below, you'll learn about two powerful advocates and how they manifested their individual impact to create meaningful change, as well as the sobering beginning of one of the greatest movements of our time. While their field of advocacy may be unconventional, think about how you can take their insights and apply them to your own life to advocate toward something you believe in.

MANNING UP TO ADVOCACY: JEFF PERERA'S STORY

What does it mean to be a man? Often the traits associated with dominance and power are those which we would categorize under the idea of masculinity. I was no exception to this preconceived idea. However, after speaking with advocate and speaker Jeff Perera, I learned how misguided that view truly is. Having delivered speeches and workshops to tens of thousands of people across North America, Jeff reinvents the conversation of manhood—what it means to be a man in present society—to embody the true spirit of advocacy.

Jeff credits this passion to his upbringing. He was raised in Canada by his Sri Lankan parents who emigrated from the UK. However, it was from witnessing his father's rigid, emotionally challenged behavior toward his mother that sparked his critique of manhood. Having remarked similar behaviors in the community he grew up in, he sought to change that reality.

Studying social work at Ryerson University in his thirties, Jeff began his work in creating impact. He joined the Ryerson chapter of White Ribbon, the world's largest movement of men striving to end violence against women.[151] His leadership position soon led to a full-time role with White Ribbon before he joined Next Gen Men, a nonprofit organization promoting positive masculinities, healthy relationships, and gender equity.[152] With his experience, he started a freelance business to continue spreading awareness of the harmful ideas of manhood and how to adopt healthier practices.

Jeff believes that there's a healthy and harmful way to be a man. Through society's influence, we have associated the traditional ideas of domination and control with manhood, resulting in harmful masculine energy. "That's that idea of 'I need to be the best, or I'm a loser.' So that energy, to me, the problem with that it doesn't allow us to take time and little moments to grow, to learn from mistakes to recognize what matters and what's important." For Jeff, healthy masculine energy comes from the thought that "I want to be my best, but not at the expense of other people."

While Jeff emphasizes that he doesn't romanticize the notion of every woman being perfect but admires the nurturing lessons most are taught from a young age. "At a certain point, we take away a teddy bear from a boy and we replace it, back in my day, with a war doll. But for young girls, we give them a baby doll to learn to take care of others before they even take care of themselves." To Jeff, that nurturing sense is empowering, helping children understand the impact they have on the world. But this same upbringing is missing in young boys.

---

151 "About White Ribbon," White Ribbon, accessed Aug. 5, 2020.

152 "About Us," Next Gen Men, accessed Aug. 5, 2020.

The unhealthy ladder of manhood is one fixated on the need to show strength and refuse help. This idea that anything less is considered weak or soft, feminine if you will, is one that Jeff actively seeks to challenge. "As men, we're trying to attain this impossible idea of manhood. It's always rooted in this notion that 'you need to be better than everyone.' You need the biggest six-pack, have the biggest car. You need to be big and you need to be the best." Jeff explains how men's entire worth is often wrapped up in the power they hold, their value and self-identity nothing more than a presentation of what they own and produce.

According to the American Psychological Association, masculine ideals such as restricting one's emotions and conforming to behaviors of dominance can increase the likelihood that men will engage in acts of violence. Especially if these behaviors begin from a young age, this dangerous idea of manhood perpetuates violence in many forms including bullying, assault, and verbal aggression. Despite these risks, as the American Psychological Association recommends, prevention strategies meant to identify these behaviors early are instrumental to long-term change. In Jeff's case, he sought to do just that and bring awareness to these harmful behaviors in children early on.[153]

Jeff strives to help guide young men to a better, more sustainable path. In 2016, he taught at a private school in Oakville, Ontario, where people send their sons to be executives or diplomats. At the time, Jeff was running an after-school

---

153 American Psychological Association, "Harmful Masculinity and Violence," *American Psychological Association*, Sept. 2018.

discussion group. Amid the US elections. the topic of discussion was Trump. When one of the kids in the group believed it was "cool" to have your name on everything like a cartoon villain, Jeff wanted to make a point that true personal value goes beyond this perception of power. He provided that Trump may seem to have power and wealth, but the controversy he's spread through his actions and character has caused strife to him and those around him. With this, he taught that compassion is a true leadership trait, and empathy is not a weakness but a great source of strength. "The measure of a man is not what we own, but rather how we serve, how we give, and how we live."

Without shaming men for the biases imposed upon them by society, Jeff guides them toward this new idea of manhood, fostering supportive discussions to invite them to be vulnerable. The mindset that he hopes to foster in others is one not rooted in competition but personal growth. There is much to learn from patience, gratitude, and grace. "Something truly impactful in your life is something you grow; you plant those seeds, you nurture it, and it takes time," he explains. And Jeff uses this to testify his view of how small actions can make a big difference.

"Sometimes it's the small little incremental steps that are so powerful. The kind of the irony of that is that those little things we do in our everyday interactions, those quiet moments, are what can ultimately lead to a change that's bigger than your lifetime."

Jeff's current goal? To create a future without violence and a place where men can contribute to healing and growth. While it's a long journey that might not be achieved in his lifetime, he's doing all that he can to plant those seeds and build the foundation for future generations.

"Rather than looking at it as this monumental goal, it's recognizing that it's still little ripples every day in our life that makes that happen."

Some of the simple acts that Jeff suggests are based around his concept of Mindful Masculinity. He explains that something any man can do to adopt a healthier approach to manhood is by listening during conversations, creating an environment where everyone can feel comfortable to speak and show vulnerability.

Jeff believes that this impact has waves. By being a positive role model to other men and fostering an environment where they can be validly vulnerable, they can do the same unto others, ultimately shifting our dynamic away from the unhealthy version of manhood into something focused on compassionate growth.

Equipped with this mindset, Jeff's efforts to create impact have been seen with great success. "I've also had people reach out to me on social media and say, 'I heard you give a talk years ago' or you 'came to my school.' People come back to me and talk about how it was an opportunity for them to sit back and think about how they contribute to the world or the way they impact their relationships and work environment.'"

Especially now, Jeff believes that we're in a time where people's truths have surfaced, whether that be through the outcry of the black community or the countries struggling with poverty. But similarly, what also surfaces are our attitudes about it.

"It's a crossroads where we can go one way or the other. We either go 'that's your problem,' or 'what can I do to help.' The world is kind of teetering on that kind of edge, but it's really up to us. The problem is when we think, 'oh, but good people will prevail.' Goodness will only prevail once you contribute and do your part."

Powerfully, Jeff speaks to the concept of Everyday Impact. If everyone were to subscribe to the idea that we should let someone else do it, then no one will get it done. It is only in everyone working for the common good that we can create a large-scale impact.

***

At the end of our interview, Jeff described an exercise he does during his training called the "empathy toss." He sits the audience in theater-style rows each holding a ball, with a recycling bin in the front of the room. After telling them to think of their ball as their dream, he tells them that they must throw their ball into the bin for it to come true.

The catch? They only have this one shot.

At the count of three, everyone tries to shoot their ball into the bin with varying results. While the front row resoundingly affirmed that it was easy for them, the back rows expressed unanimous frustration, complaining that the people in front blocked their shot. With this, he forces the audience to consider their privilege or disadvantage, to be aware of how each of them impacts another in this space. For example, ducking to give someone behind you a clear view of the bin doesn't affect your shot, but it makes a huge difference for the other person. Think about your advantage and how you can help others with it. When everyone helps each other, we all have a better shot of getting our ball in the recycling bin.

"It's not about being better than everyone else. It's about being better than your yesterdays." Emphasizing the importance of self-improvement and collaboration in true societal change, Jeff encourages others to do their part to contribute to shaping a better world, one man at a time.

From Jeff's story, we see how meaningful change is only possible through consistent actions and being willing to stand up and support the things you believe in which are important to society, regardless of whether they are controversial. With the rise of technology and exponential growth of social media, our current society presents unprecedented opportunities for advocacy and sharing our thoughts. As we introduced in the beginning, advocacy can be anything from changing the discussion on a controversial topic or as simple as posting updates about world issues to raise awareness on current problems.

As we'll explore in the story below, most of you reading this book now are in unique positions of advocacy potential. It is important to be aware of your privilege and opportunities, and with that knowledge, use them as a force of good.

GIVING VALUABLE VOICE TO UNCOMFORTABLE DISCUSSIONS

Leigh Naturkach is a professional in philanthropy, public and individual giving, and corporate partnerships with a special focus on health care and social justice organizations. She is a passionate community engagement member with expertise in the feminist, death literacy, and advocacy space. While Leigh has received great success throughout her professional career, her work in the impact and advocacy space is what truly stands out in her story.

Leigh started in media career at Corus Entertainment working on many different channels from numerous positions. She learned about the different levels of an organization and developed key skills in marketing, storytelling, and production that she uses today.

Yet in her early career, the two passions she identified with most were social justice and the women's movement. In 2008, Leigh made the switch to the nonprofit by joining the

Canadian Women's Foundation.[154] "I had about maybe 40 percent of what I needed to do that first job and 60 percent of 'I have no idea.' I just sort of jumped off the ship there and went for it."

A defining characteristic about Leigh is her unique and uncommon trait of not falling to the pressures of the professional climate. "There is that pressure to feel like you have to rise this ladder to take this next step," Leigh confesses, but she deliberately chose not to follow the conventional path. "There were these wonderful things that were coming my way. But I realized I needed to take stock of what gives me joy, what keeps me attached to the work. And it wasn't more of the executive management pieces."

Leigh wasn't interested in simply making management decisions and influencing others indirectly from the top of the hierarchy. She yearned for something beyond a fancy title, seeking to be on the ground where she could make a tangible and active difference herself. Rather than focusing on promotion, she actively chose paths that fit with her values and purposeful goals.

Another one of Leigh's greatest traits is her sincere awareness of her privilege, which she actively uses to guide her decisions. Coming from a solid family, Leigh recalls that she was lucky to have access to great opportunities in life, not needing to worry about barriers such as skin color or socioeconomic factors. She considers the ability to choose a privilege and remains mindful of that.

---

154 "About Us," Canadian Women's Foundation, accessed Aug. 5, 2020.

For Leigh, she places a major emphasis on the importance of values in one's career. "What I realized is that you don't have to walk away from everything just because it doesn't align perfectly all the time. It's about how you can work to make those spaces more aligned with your values." Leigh advises to choose your top five values and reflect upon how you can act upon them in your personal and professional life.

She regards her most prominent value to be advocacy. As a major proponent of bringing awareness to issues that are less talked about, she recommends that everyone be curious and critical of the organization that they work for and interact with. While there are a lot of complicated things in the world to handle, Leigh remarked kindly that "I think that's why I love the purpose of your book detailing what you can do every day. It's about where we start with what we have right now."

With the Canadian Women's Foundation, Leigh managed a campaign called Women Moving Women—a $6 million fundraising campaign—as her first job in the philanthropy world. This was a national campaign launched in 2008 that funded economic development programs for low-income women. It focused on galvanizing a movement across the country on awareness and support for this issue. Despite the grandeur of the project, Leigh embraced the challenge, and a major source of motivation was the beauty that came from seeing the collaboration of this collective goal.

"There are twenty-five hundred women across the country who each collectively donated to be part of this collective whole." As much as Leigh learned from mega-philanthropists, she was even more inspired by the generosity of the women at lower income levels who ended up giving more. "And so when you think of someone giving half of what they have left on Earth to another person just because they know what it's like, that kind of inspiration is very humbling and you just think 'I can always do more.'"

Leigh's main involvement and where her advocacy shines is in the death and dying space. Her passion began when she served on the board of the Women's Reproductive Choice organization which got her interested in the specifics of grief: how a culture understands death, how we learn to grieve, and how grief manifests. This started a decade-long journey for Leigh in raising awareness about this lesser-discussed topic. She sought to spark new ways of thinking by challenging people to talk about death and dying openly.

"In the area of legacy, our work is made up of everyday acts, everyday conversations, everyday things that we do. But the result is this beautiful, intricate impact that we've left in the world."

Leigh described such daily commitments and small acts as encompassed in her job of spreading awareness. As an advocate, Leigh actively sparked discussions with people like her own husband who was very death averse. But by engaging him to have these conversations, she's been able to get him to open up to the topic and even get his will done. And in her community, she has been able to increase death and grief literacy. "It's these droplets that have kind of grown over time," Leigh admits. "I think people look to me now to have those conversations and to understand the different ways that they wouldn't before." Commendably, Leigh has been able to dispel some of the apprehension toward an important but previously taboo subject.

For me, Leigh's story is especially unique as I'd never personally engaged with anyone who's actually in the death and dying space, a personal realization of which only emphasized how these topics are considered akin to taboo in our society. I would compare this to subjects of mental health only a few years ago, as mental disorders were issues that people traditionally found to be forbidden topics of discussion.

However, as we've seen from the surge of mental health advocates, it has since become one of the most important topics today. It was always a major issue, but it took people who were willing to speak out against the counterintuitive norm of silencing these "depressing" subjects to give it the platform it deserved. As a labor of love, it is a challenging but necessary process to create meaningful change.

"The point of me entering the death and dying space was not for career ambition," Leigh explained. "It's about how I contribute to society, and your career is one way of doing that."

Making maps, not monuments. This is what Leigh believes to best encompass the leadership style in this space of social justice work. In advocacy, this mindset is evident as spreading awareness for what you believe in is what will set the model example for others.

The most meaningful work is being done in uncomfortable places, and it is only in normalizing those conversations that people who are left most vulnerable through those issues can receive the support they need. "I feel like the unmentionable is what needs to be talked about. That helps to reduce stigma, it helps normalize experiences, develop understanding, and allow everyone to navigate the world in a better way."

Leigh's career has been fueled by active engagement, evolution, and advocacy. Through these common themes, Leigh has been able to connect each of her experiences while using the skills and experiences she gained from each to enrich and deepen her involvement with others. In the same way, I hope that you will be able to implement those themes into your own life and speak out for what is right.

CONSISTENCY IN ADVOCACY: THE RISE AND GROWTH OF THE BLACK LIVES MATTER MOVEMENT

Beyond individual stories, even the growth of collective movements is done in incremental stages. Consistent actions of advocacy, even if small, can make a big difference.

Change is not often a product of a single event or individual. True change is done when people come together and fight for what they believe in. Often, that gathering comes as a result of an outcry to change something we deem to be unacceptable. One of the most well-known movements of the twenty-first century came as a result of that very notion.

In 2012, a tragedy in Sanford, Florida sparked a movement that would have unprecedented consequences. On February 26, seventeen-year-old Black teenager Trayvon Martin was shot and killed on the way home from a convenience store by George Zimmerman, a neighborhood watch volunteer. The Miami high school student had been returning home after purchasing a bag of Skittles and a bottle of juice from the store when Zimmerman saw him and, given the recent series of break-ins around the neighborhood, deemed him to be suspicious.[155]

After informing the police of his suspicion, Zimmerman pursued Martin against the police's advice. It was only moments later that gunfire resounded across the neighborhood.

Martin was dead when the police arrived.

Zimmerman sported a bloody nose and a few cuts to the head. When he claimed to have acted in self-defense, he was promptly let go without trouble from the police. It was only after Martin's parents raised concerns around the lack of police investigation that the case gained traction. Less than a month later, protest rallies were held across America as then President Barack Obama declared that, "If I had a son, he would look like Trayvon."[156]

It was nearly two months after that Zimmerman was charged with second-degree murder, and it was another year later on July 13 that Zimmerman was found not guilty. It was the news

155 Orlando Sentinel, "Florida Teen Trayvon Martin is Shot and Killed," *History*, Feb. 26, 2012.

156 Ibid.

of this acquittal that started the now renowned movement known as #BlackLivesMatter (BLM).[157]

This political and Black-centered movement was organized by Alicia Garza, Patrisse Cullors, and Opal Tometi. The movement developed a space and platform bringing to light the racial discrimination and oppression that persists in the twenty-first century while being used to amplify against and advocate for anti-racism for the Black community.

It has since grown to become a global organization called Black Lives Matter Global Network Foundation with a mission to intervene in violence against Black communities and dismantle white supremacy. The global network is made up of chapters organized by members aiming to stand up for Black lives and rights in a world with systemic racism.[158]

When the movement was fueled again in 2014 with the murder of Mike Brown by Ferguson police officer Darren Wilson, the BLM Movement grew again. Soon after, the organization's infrastructure was developed with an explicit set of guiding principles to support new Black leaders and foster a network for Black people to regain control over their lives.[159]

The BLM Movement wouldn't have had the impact it had if it was truly just a "trend." Certainly, consistent actions and constant advocacy is what brought it to the forefront. Indeed, the advocacy and fight for Black rights and empowerment

157 "About," Black Lives Matter, accessed Sept. 23, 2020

158 Ibid.

159 "Herstory," Black Lives Matter, accessed Sept. 23, 2020.

never stopped. The constant sparks of this movement were doused with a gallon of kerosene oil in June of 2020.

On May 25, forty-six-year-old Black man George Floyd was arrested after buying cigarettes with an allegedly counterfeit $20 bill. Seventeen minutes after the police arrived, Mr. Floyd was held beneath three police officers, showing no signs of life. Videos soon surfaced of what had occurred; a horrific showing of officers pinning Mr. Floyd down and Derek Chauvin keeping his knee on his neck for eight minutes and fifteen seconds while he and onlookers called for help. Tragically, Mr. Floyd died that day. The police department fired all four officers involved, and charges were placed upon the actors. However, this injustice spoke for much more. This was a clear showing of unjustified police brutality against the Black community, and the entire nation was outraged.[160]

On June 6, five hundred thousand people protested in nearly five hundred fifty places across the US. People rose in the streets and online to stand in solidarity with the Black community as the #BlackLivesMatter movement resurged at the top of virtually all social media channels. This was a movement that shook the very recesses of the country, expanding to reach networks around the world.[161]

Recent studies from the data science firm Civis Analytics working with business and Democratic campaigns show that

---

160 Eval Hill et al., "How George Floyd was Killed in Police Custody," *The New York Times*, May 31, 2020.

161 Larry Buchanan, Quoctrung But, and Jugal K. Patel, "Black Lives Matter May Be the Largest Movement in U.S. History," *The New York Times,* July 3, 2020.

fifteen million to twenty-six million people in the US were participants in the demonstrations over George Floyd and others' death during the weeks in June. Such numbers would make this the largest movement in US history.[162]

Beyond citizens, corporations and organizations became involved in the support. From the NFL to Ben & Jerry's to the popular K-pop group BTS, their presence encouraged supporters and brought attention to those who would've otherwise sat on the sidelines.[163]

Most importantly, the change that the movement rallied was not insignificant. The City Council of Minneapolis pledged the dismantling of its police department as New York lawmakers repealed a law that previously kept police disciplinary records hidden from the public eye. Laws banning chokeholds sprouted across the country, and Mississippi retired their state flag which had previously included a Confederate battle emblem.[164]

"It looks, for all the world, like these protests are achieving what very few do: setting in motion a period of significant, sustained, and widespread social, political change," said emeritus professor Douglas McAdam of Stanford University who studies social movements. "We appear to be

---

162 Ibid.

163 Ibid.

164 Luis Ferré-Sadurní and Jesse McKinley, "N.Y. Bans Chokeholds and Approves Other Measures to Restrict Police," *The New York Times*, June 17, 2020.

experiencing a social change tipping point—that is as rare in society as it is potentially consequential."[165]

While the BLM Movement may have seemed sudden, it was only a match falling on a haystack that had already accumulated over the years. Indeed, change is not created overnight; it is the product of consistent action and support for the issues we believe in.

It was not one organization that created such immense change. No, it was the coming together of organizations and individuals, of nonprofits and businesses uniting in a single cause to create the change that was long overdue.

TAKEAWAYS

"Rome was not built in a day."[166] In the same way, true social change is rarely if ever something that can happen overnight. Change takes time and effort and building a movement starts with small actions, just as building a prosperous city is a brick-by-brick process.

While the thought of putting oneself out there can be daunting, the beauty of impact and advocacy alike is its variance and flexibility. Advocacy can present itself in different ways, whether that's through speaking tours and presentations like Jeff, formulating discussion in the community like Leigh or contributing to spreading awareness for movements like BLM.

---

165 Larry Buchanan et al., "Black Lives Matter May Be the Largest Movement in U.S. History," July 3, 2020.

166 "Rome Wasn't Built in a Day," The Phrase Finder, accessed Sept. 5, 2020.

Ultimately, advocacy is how we can make our voices heard. Consistency is key to change. And everyday advocacy is what it takes to shape the world we want to see.

CHAPTER 8

SOCIAL ENTREPRENEURSHIP & THE IMPACT OF BUSINESS

———

My fundamental philosophy is one of abundance. There is more than enough love, generosity, hope, talent, money and resources in the world—if only we would all commit to sharing them more equitably.

—JAN OWEN, CEO OF THE FOUNDATION
FOR YOUNG AUSTRALIANS[167]

The corporate world has undergone many changes. While I grew up with the image of business as the field dominated by powerful profit-hungry figures, this narrative has

———

167 Alexandra Nemeth, "Quotes from Social Entrepreneurs to Inspire You to Change the World," *Social Enterprise* (blog), *MovingWorlds,* Nov. 25, 2019.

shifted as businesses are less seen as instigators for social issues and increasingly regarded as tools for problem-solving and impact.

In this era of massive modern growth, the business world is radically changing. Not only have these positive developments changed my life and shaped my future path, but it has done the same for many others.

THE GUIDING PATH OF SOCIAL ENTREPRENEURSHIP

In life, we strive for fulfilment. For young social entrepreneur Tiffany Yau, she took that idea literally. As the founder of the organization "Fulphil," Tiffany found empowerment from social entrepreneurship and seeks to educate under-resourced youth in Philadelphia about the field's incredible potential.[168] However, Tiffany did not follow such a linear route to get to where she is now.

Tiffany attended college at the University of Pennsylvania (Penn) as an undergraduate to pursue her childhood dream: saving lives and making a difference. While her upbringing led her down a path of medicine, when she began to study biology and chemistry, she became overwhelmed, quickly realizing that it may not be the path for her. Despite the implicit pressure from other students who all seemed to be scrambling for a job, Tiffany made an important decision; rather than looking for a job in something she didn't enjoy, she wanted to find what she liked doing first.

---

168 "Home," Fulphil, accessed Aug. 26, 2020.

She began to study sociology, as she cared deeply about social issues and understanding why things are the way that they are. From learning about human interaction in society, she began to understand issues ranging from poverty to health care and equity.

She first encountered the term *social entrepreneurship* through the Hult Prize Foundation, an organization seeking to empower social entrepreneurs on a global scale. The organization hosted an accelerated competition for university students to solve the world's most pressing social challenges through social entrepreneurship. In her junior year, Tiffany got involved as a marketing director and became a campus director the next year. From there, she learned about the role of social entrepreneurship in changing the world.

In 2016, the theme for Penn's school year was the refugee crisis. As Tiffany specialized in human interaction, she innovated through entrepreneurship, using her past knowledge to show people a new, sociological understanding of the problem. "You have to understand the problems to be able to get a good solution," She explained. As such, Tiffany got a Syrian refugee from Philadelphia to share his story with fellow students. Seeing the tangible impact that his story had on other people inspired Tiffany. She saw the potential of social entrepreneurship in changing perspectives and improving lives, and she was invested.

Tiffany applied for a master's in nonprofit leadership at Penn's School of Social Policy & Practice with a hope to create something that would empower youth to create impact. Soon after her acceptance, Tiffany was informed that her Hult Prize competition in her program received recognition for being one of the top twenty in the world that year. She was invited to attend the Hult Prize competition in Ashridge, London. There, she found herself sitting next to the CEO of the foundation during a dinner.

In a bout of courage and determination, she decided to pitch an idea to the CEO to create an all-Ivy League platform for Hult Prize. This encounter got Tiffany her first job as an international accelerator for the foundation to develop her idea into the Hult Prize Ivy initiative challenging over one thousand Ivy League students in solving the world's social issues.

"I think it was just one of those moments; when someone gives you an opportunity, trusts you with it and actually lets you do it, that changes your perspective on how you think about things."

That summer, Tiffany was motivated to start something that she could call her own.

She explained that in Philadelphia, over 25 percent of the population live in poverty with little access to education or resources. Coupled with admiration for the Hult Prize's mission of exposing young people to social entrepreneurship, she realized there was a lack of entrepreneurship education for students in under-resourced neighborhoods and sought to teach students social entrepreneurship on a local level. She believed that social entrepreneurship could catalyze economic development and wanted to share this belief with other young residents.

The idea was also born out of a realization that many people come to the city of Philadelphia, get their education and live out some of the most transformative years of their lives, but leave without giving back. This didn't sit right with Tiffany who, even being from Southern California herself, still felt a need to give back to the community which shaped her life moving forward.

"At the time, I knew nothing about starting anything. But I was hungry to learn, to watch, read, just to figure out how you start something," Tiffany explained. She successfully founded a nonprofit called Fulphil which would bring social entrepreneurship education to under-resourced students. The social venture started small, beginning as a dorm-room side hustle. It has since grown to employ over fifteen employees and thirty changemakers serving high schools in Philadelphia.[169]

Fulphil offers accessible social entrepreneurship education to high school students. It has since taught over three thousand youths to create startup ideas benefiting their local communities. They also created a five-week accelerator program where over thirty speakers from a variety of industries work with students to build a problem-solving framework for community issues.[170]

The purpose of Fulphil's programs and social entrepreneurship curriculum is to provide students with the capacity to

---

169 "My Story," Tiffany Yau, accessed Aug. 14, 2020.

170 Khai Tran, "Bringing Entrepreneurship Education to Students in Under-served Communities: Interview with Tiffany Yau," *Forbes*, Jan. 16, 2020.

choose their own path. Through social entrepreneurship, Tiffany was able to find her calling. Now, she uses it to inspire new generations of changemakers to "fulphil" the needs of their community.

INSPIRE & ENGAGE THROUGH SOCIAL ENTREPRENEURSHIP

This same trend of social entrepreneurship as a guiding path is consistent across many inspiring individuals. Like Tiffany, another young social entrepreneur named Melody Hossaini uses the field to guide her impact while leveraging her past hardships as a springboard for change.

Melody was born in Tehran, Iran, in 1984 during the Gulf War. She is a war refugee, an asylum seeker whose earliest memories consist of bombs and violence. Her family fled to Sweden where she grew up and, influenced by the horrors of her early life, became passionate about social justice. Later on, their family moved again to South Staffordshire in the UK, where she attended Great Wyrley High School. There, she was severely bullied and subjected to racist behaviors.[171]

Despite her mistreatment, she learned early on fighting fire with fire would only prolong the pain on both ends; the only way to heal was to invest positive energy in others. At the age of thirteen, she sought opportunities to make a difference and do something greater. This led to her co-founding the UK Youth Parliament, where she worked hard to rally

---

171 *TEDx Talks,* "The Social Enterprise Revolution: Melody Hossaini at TEDxKLWomen 2013," Mar. 24, 2014, Video, 17:49.

supporters toward the cause of social justice. Overcoming its small beginnings, it soon grew into the world's most successful democratic youth organization.[172]

In 2006, she obtained an Honors law degree from Oxford Brookes University and decided to follow her passion in the youth sector. From then on, she became a social entrepreneur and started InspirEngage International, a social enterprise with a portfolio in over 100 countries and reaching over 1 million people.[173]

Social entrepreneurship allowed Melody to find her calling in life. She believes herself to be a Human Investor. At InspirEngage International, she and her colleagues have learned that "magic happens when you invest in human potential." Melody and InspirEngage offered various programs for females of all ages on talent retention for corporates and empowering young ambitions. "Be bold in what you want to make you happy, seek opportunities that offer the balance, and stay connected to your purpose," she recommends. As she continued to empower generations of women, Melody became the first social entrepreneur on BBC's *The Apprentice* in 2011 and won the Women of the Future Award among others.[174]

Melody is a proponent of social changes in business and believes that the future of work will be driven by innovation. She describes the positive changing dynamics of the

---

172 Ibid.

173 Ibid.

174 Exeleon, "Melody Hossaini: Transforming Lives by Harvesting Human Potentials," *Exeleon Magazine,* (n.d.).

business world, where we are increasingly aware and keeping people accountable in business. Indeed, we are moving from a competitive world to a collaborative one.[175]

To this end, Melody speaks to the beautiful potential of social enterprise.

"Social enterprise is when your head and your heart work together."

—MELODY

This is a new dimension of business, and Melody believes that the old "dog-eat-dog" world that we'd known before is now making way for people with heart.[176]

Based on her knowledge and personal experiences, Melody believes that social enterprises are born when our chips are down, just as the greatest changes in our world have come as a response to urgent challenges. Indeed, is important to reflect upon your past experiences, find your identity, and take action to express your unique and purposeful selves.[177]

Having personally benefited from the life-changing influence of social entrepreneurship, she believes that we need to give young people similar opportunities and insight to flourish.

---

175 TEDx Talks, "The Social Enterprise Revolution," Mar. 24, 2014.

176 Ibid.

177 Ibid.

"Growth . . . is being led by young people because they're finding it as a bridge from volunteering into a career. So something they're passionate about, that they've been building up expertise and networks in, is now becoming a real transition where they can set themselves as a business, make a difference, and make money. The perfect model."[178]

As Melody and Tiffany's stories show, social entrepreneurship has helped the lives of the entrepreneur and all those that their services have helped, effectively producing a wonderful ripple effect of impact. Personally, the proof is undeniable, testifying the dynamic changes of the business world that can only lead to greater potential.

WITH GREAT POWER COMES GREAT RESPONSIBILITY

As we noted in the beginning, the image of business is gradually changing, but I recognize how it may be difficult to shake off that ingrained image of the *Wolf of Wall Street*. Since the best way to learn something is through repetition, I will provide more examples of how for-profit businesses have been going above-and-beyond to implement social impact in their operations. Beyond nonprofits and social enterprises, we must also acknowledge the power of corporations in creating positive social change. In doing so, it opens a world of greater potential.

---

178 *Melody Hossaini,* "Advancement of Young People & Women in Social Enterprise," Oct. 19, 2015, Video, 3:07.

Michael Porter, an American academic and economist, is the most cited scholar in economics and business. Known for his work in competitive strategy, Porter is also outspoken about the greater potential of business in contributing to social efforts. As he states, we tend to see business as a problem. Admittedly, there have been plenty of bad actors that we've seen throughout history, with most literature being focused on the view of business as profit-maximizing machines sans emotional values. However, Porter rejects this view and believes that businesses should be seen as solutions to social efforts.[179]

***

The past few decades have shown a tremendous rise in NGOs and philanthropy. Put together, we tend to associate solutions as being exclusive to NGOs and governments. Porter himself was no exception, as his previous methodology was to create a nonprofit each time he sought a solution to a social problem. Despite creating four nonprofits, Porter cites that this has created an "awkward reality."[180]

"We're not making fast enough progress. We're not winning," he stated. Despite the establishment of nonprofit organizations, the result was not as impactful as he anticipated.[181]

179 "Michael E. Porter," Harvard Business School, accessed Aug. 28, 2020.

180 *TED,* "Michael Porter: Why Business Can Be Good at Solving Social Problems," Oct. 7, 2013, Video, 16:28.

181 Ibid.

Digging to the root of this problem, Porter explains that the problem lies with scale. The current model for nonprofits is lacking in resources and capital to deal with pressing problems. As the scarcity of dealing with those problems continue to grow, the presence of such resources in traditional for-profit business becomes more noticeable.[182]

According to Porter, "All wealth is actually created by business." In the US, corporations hold $20.1 trillion of total revenue by stakeholder compared to the government and nonprofit sector's 3.1 trillion and 1.2 trillion respectively. Businesses hold so much power and resources, yet we're still leaving much of that area untapped.[183]

The conventional wisdom is that business makes profit by causing social problems, or that sustainable alternatives are more time and money costly. However, this is a very simplistic view. Deeper analyses show that businesses may actually profit from solving social issues. This can come in the form of consumers being attracted by a firm that has adopted sustainable packaging to an organization that provides greater health benefits for its employees so that their workers can come to work and be more productive.[184]

"There is no trade-off between social progress and economic efficiency in any fundamental sense."[185]

---

182 Ibid.

183 Ibid.

184 Ibid.

185 Ibid.

As a consumer, I can say that socially responsible practices are major selling points for young people. I feel good buying from a company that I know cares for its stakeholders. When companies go above-and-beyond in demonstrating their social consciousness, the previous image of these companies as profit-maximizing capitalist tools is dispelled, allowing for greater customer loyalty.

In this way, consistent with the growth of NGOs and social impact-focused organizations, more companies have begun to adopt purpose-based initiatives. These sustainable and CSR-friendly practices have created numerous "win-win" situations, providing companies with positive exposure while delivering meaningful impact to their stakeholders.

In the stories below, you will learn about the unique initiatives that companies have planned and hopefully gain a greater appreciation for the power of corporations in creating meaningful change.

THE POWER OF PURPOSEFUL PLAY

Over the past decade, Lego has been consistently considered as one of the companies with the greatest corporate responsibility reputations in the world. According to the Reputation Institute, a reputation measurement and management services firm, Lego was ranked first in the world for Corporate Responsibility (CR) in their 2019 CR reputation study.[186]

---

186 Vicky Valet, "The World's Most Reputable Companies for Corporate Responsibility 2019." *Forbes*, Sept. 17, 2019.

Lego's commitment to social responsibility is highly effective and innovative. Their initiatives are all fitting with their brand image as they seek to implement measures to empower children and bring about learning through play. Notably, it has recently announced the arrival of Lego Braille Bricks to cater to consumers with sight disabilities.[187] Lego has also partnered with organizations like the Ellen MacArthur Foundation to accelerate the move toward a circular economy, investing $400 million over three years for sustainability efforts.[188]

What makes Lego's approach to business so effective is that they have essentially harmonized their products with an explicit commitment to social responsibility. Everything is cohesive and fitting with their fundamental mission of putting children first and championing the power of learning through play to inspire builders of tomorrow. This core message of learning through play is in itself simple but powerful.[189]

"No company has demonstrated its commitment to corporate responsibility quite like Lego," commented a *Forbes* article on the world's most reputable companies for CSR in 2019.

"Last year, Lego started producing pieces made from plant-based polyethene, the first of many steps toward achieving its mission of making all bricks sustainable by

---

187 "About Lego Braille Bricks," Lego Braille Bricks, accessed Aug. 27, 2020.

188 Lego, "Ellen MacArthur Foundation and LEGO Group Join Forces to Accelerate the Move Towards a Circular Economy," *Lego*, Aug. 30, 2020.

189 "Learning Through Play," Lego Braille Bricks, accessed Aug. 14, 2020.

2030. The company also came within seven percentage points of reaching its goal of recycling 100 percent of its operational waste by 2025. It also was ahead of schedule in meeting its target of generating as much renewable energy as its business consumes—doing so by means of investments in offshore wind farms in Germany and the United Kingdom."[190]

According to the chief reputation officer of the Reputation Institute, "Lego has raised the bar in its commitment to the planet of tomorrow. It has made corporate responsibility a priority for the company, and it's implicit in everything it does."[191]

MAKING YOUR IMPACT AND EATING IT TOO

Ben & Jerry's is one of the most beloved ice cream brands in America. While much of their notoriety comes from their unique flavors like "Netflix and Chill'd", many customers were drawn in by something other than their sweet tooth: the brand's commitment to community impact.[192]

Ben & Jerry's came from humble beginnings. It started from a $5 course on ice cream, where childhood friends Ben Cohen and Jerry Greenfield were inspired to open an ice cream shop in Burlington, Vermont, with just $12,000 in investment cash. Now, their products can be found in grocery stores across

190 Vicky Valet, "The World's Most Reputable Companies for Corporate Responsibility 2019," Forbes, Sept. 17, 2019.

191 Ibid.

192 "Our History," Ben & Jerry's, accessed Aug. 15, 2020.

America. Throughout their growth, a major point that Ben & Jerry's kept consistent in addition to its quality flavor is its commitment to improving its communities.[193]

In 1985, they established the Ben & Jerry's Foundation, pledging 7.5 percent of annual pre-tax profits for community-oriented projects. Then in 1992, the company joined a cooperative campaign with the nonprofit Children's Defense Fund dedicated to bringing the issue of basic needs for vulnerable children to the forefront of the national agenda. From 2005 onward, Ben & Jerry's manifested their impact in unique ways: They constructed a 900-pound Baked Alaska with their Fossil Fuel ice cream in protest of the oil drilling in the Arctic National Wildlife Refuge. In 2019, they delivered ice cream in New York City to support protestors rallying against increased economic inequality. In 2015, it even introduced a new ice cream flavor to complement its activism campaign known as the "Save Our Swirled" to stand against climate change.[194]

"Without question, the balance of power on the planet today lies in the hands of business. Corporations rival governments in wealth, influence, and power. Indeed, business all too often pulls the strings of government. Competing institutions—religion, the press, even the military—play subordinate roles in much of the world today. If a values-driven approach to business can begin to redirect this vast power toward more

---

193 Ibid.

194 Ibid.

constructive ends than the simple accumulation of wealth, the human race and Planet Earth will have a fighting chance."

—BEN COHEN, CO-FOUNDER OF BEN & JERRY'S, AUTHOR OF *VALUES-DRIVEN BUSINESS: HOW TO CHANGE THE WORLD, MAKE MONEY, AND HAVE FUN*[195]

***

Ultimately, these primary examples are indicative of the potential for business to both benefit the world and themselves through social responsibility initiatives, proving that business can create a societal impact while boosting their own growth through the years.

FROM GOOD TO GREAT: CAPITALIZING ON THE POWER OF PRIVATE TO MAKE PUBLIC IMPACT

Beyond organizations, individuals have the power to inspire organizational change. For innovator Ann Mei Chang, she used her experience in the private sector to inspire public sector impact.

Ann is the executive director of the US Global Development Lab at the United States Agency for International Development (USAID), a bureau merging twenty-first century technology and innovations to accelerate global development. She also served as the chief innovation officer for the NGO Mercy Corps and the senior advisor for women and technology in

---

195 Ibid.

the Secretary's Office of Global Women's Issues at the US Department of State.[196]

Before her public sector engagement, Ann Mei worked in Silicon Valley for companies including Google and Apple for over twenty years. It was this prior experience that led her to a unique method of approaching impact in both the public and private sector.[197]

Ann studied as a software engineer and became an engineering director at Google, leading mobile teams to build apps like Google Maps and Gmail for mobile phones. But throughout her tech career, she wanted to do something more meaningful. When she switched to lead a new group focused on emerging markets, she joined a state department delegation to Liberia and Sierra Leone. There, she saw firsthand how difficult life was for native residents. But notably, she also witnessed how aid and charity programs were only reaching a fraction of those in need.[198]

After the trip, Ann struggled to find a way to contribute. As she explored the public sector and looked at the ways that people were addressing prevalent societal issues, she learned immense challenges were being worked on by amazing people and fueled by incredible resources. But despite all these

---

196 "Biography," Ann Mei Chang, accessed July 13, 2020.

197 Ibid.

198 *TEDx Talks*, "Ending Global Poverty: Let's Think Like Silicon Valley | Ann Mei Chang | TEDxMidAtlantic," Jan. 10, 2017, Video, 12:24.

inputs, Ann felt like the output was not creating the change we needed.[199]

In 2011, Ann left Google to work toward social good; specifically, toward alleviating global poverty using a new social change approach that would bring together the private and public sector.

"I think my journey over the last eight years has been trying to figure out not how I can make my own tiny little mark on some corner of some issue, but looking at the system and saying, 'how can we do this better.' Trying to bring some of my experiences from Google and other places to some of these big social challenges."[200]

Accordingly, Ann fell back on her experience in Silicon Valley to define a new way for impact.

***

Research testifies to the fact that private investment is blossoming. More attention shines on private sector development on how it can be leveraged to promote social changes such as poverty reduction, sustainability, and equitable economic growth. The organization GSDRC has produced a topic guide depicting the evidence of private sector development work on social impact.

---

199 Ibid.

200 *Talks at Google,* "Radical Innovation for Greater Social Good | Ann Mei Chang | Talks at Google," Feb. 19, 2019, Video, 55:01.

"As a creator of jobs and producer of goods and services that poor people use, the private sector can have a transformational impact on people's lives. Making use of social development thinking is essential to effective private sector development work that is responsible, inclusive, and delivers sustainable benefits to poor people."[201]

Ann explains how global development programs are measured in terms of tens or hundreds of thousands of people reached. "In Silicon Valley, my success was defined in terms of reaching tens of hundreds of millions. We need that kind of scale if we're going to end global poverty!" she exclaimed.[202]

We needed a new set of rules to generate impact, with the first step to be catalytic by engaging private and local government investment as charity only represents 2 percent of spending. So how do we reach these two groups?[203]

Ann explains this process using the story of Off-Grid Electric, a company that installs home solar systems for Tanzania. It began as an idea from Erica Mackey, an American student living in Tanzania who wanted to help the 85 percent of people in the country living without electricity. But how was she

---

201 "Executive Summary," GSDRC, accessed July 13, 2020.

202 TEDx Talks, "Ending Global Poverty," Jan. 10, 2017.

203 Ibid.

going to pay for this? Erica remembered that three-quarters of Tanzanians have a mobile phone with a system of mobile money, meaning that anyone could transfer money in small amounts. So she designed a new system to use mobile money to pay off one's solar systems at just a few cents a day. The new design was wildly successful, and Off-Grid now provides electricity to over one hundred thousand people.[204]

They started with a small $100,000 loan from USAID to test out their business model and received two more rounds of funding totaling $6 million for its initial success. Owing to their self-sustainable financial model, they were able to bring in over 100 million in debt and equity through private funding, allowing them to reach exponentially more people than if they had relied solely on grants.

"Aid is not going to end global poverty. But global poverty is not going to end without aid. Rather than delivering aid, we need to drive innovation to find better solutions and bring in private and local government investments so that those solutions last beyond a grant and scale to the size of the need."[205]

Ann describes this path to impact as "Lean Impact," based on the philosophy of the book *The Lean Startup* by Eric Ries that describes best practices for innovation in Silicon Valley. This methodology consists of creating products and services under circumstances of extreme uncertainty.[206]

---

204 Ibid.

205 Ibid.

206 Ibid.

Ann applies this to the social sector working on entrenched challenges that have no clear solution. Ann's "Lean Impact" consists of three fundamental paths summarized below:[207]

- **Think Big:** Be ambitious with your goals and efforts, asking yourself, "How can I make the most impact?"

- **Start Small:** Focus on delivery rather than over-planning to learn from and adapt to complex environments. Social innovation must deliver on all three buckets of Value, Impact, and Growth:

  - *Value:* Is this result something you want?

  - *Impact:* Has it delivered the expected social benefit?

  - *Growth:* Can we get it to the people and places that will benefit from it?

- **Seek Impact:** To not get distracted by the solution but to stay focused on the problem. To stay focused on measuring impact and foregoing the need to establish ownership of a solution. Instead of absolute numbers such as the number of people touched or money raised, focus on innovation metrics such as the conversion rate, success rate, the unit cost of each person reached. This will offer more clear understandings of the actual impact your organization will have.

In sum, Ann's methodology consists of having a big goal, running small experiments to see how to get there, and staying relentlessly focused throughout that process on creating the greatest impact. This methodology can be applied to any

207 *Upswell,* "Upswell 2018 (Ann Mei Chang)," Jan 17, 2019, Video, 19:36.

business, and Ann believes that it is through these steps that we can accelerate social innovation and positive change in our society.

Bringing the inspiring innovation we see from top Silicon Valley companies to the social sector, Ann imbues her past engineering experiences to social challenges, proving how the business world can be married with the social sector to create new methods of generating impact far greater than any could have achieved alone.

TAKEAWAYS

Overall, the changing business world also requires changes in its actors to produce the greatest result. Accordingly, I offer a few pieces of advice:

- For young people, you are in a unique position to start your own social enterprise similar to Tiffany and Melody, equipped with social media platforms that will help amplify our voices and beliefs. As consumers, we must continue holding companies accountable to promote positive development in the business world.

- For those searching for a career, it is important to ensure that your values align with the business that you are seeking to join. Choosing a company founded on purpose will not only provide you with a place where you can grow but enable you to benefit others in the process.

- For those seasoned workers, it is still never too late to create an impact. With your expertise, you are in the best position to bring innovative ideas to your organization while ensuring that purposeful values are implemented into its operations.

Business makes the world go round. It offers so many resources for people to tap into, but like a double-edged sword, the impact of the private sector can easily sway between the realms of negative externalities to positive social change. Since this is for us to determine, let us promote and redefine what it means to do business and show how it can not only make the world go round, but make the world a much better place to live.

CHAPTER 9

YOUNG IMPACT

——

"You won't understand until you're older."

"This isn't something a child like you should be worried about."

For young people, these are simply different variations of the same idea that we've been told for the majority of our lives. Similar to ethnicities, one's age can elicit strong preconceived notions from both peers and ourselves. These beliefs, in turn, are those which often hinder our growth.

The logic behind this is not all unfounded. Growing up in a Chinese household, it is in our culture to respect elders owing to the wisdom they possess from their greater expanse of time and life experience.

However, this mindset can be quite limiting. Especially for young ambitious students, the disseminated perception of "waiting until you're older" can be a barrier to getting to the next level.

When young people go "above-and-beyond," they may be regarded as "try-hards" by their peers or even viewed as anomalies by adults. When adults work beyond the norm, they're heralded as role models and true professionals in their field. Such varied perspectives to the same action of exceeding the norm are counterproductive and contribute to establishing a lower expectation of youth.

I believe that it's important to hold ourselves to higher standards. To believe in our abilities rather than settling with the simple roles that society pre-determined. If you keep making the excuse of waiting to grow older and expecting the experiences to flow to you on their own, those experiences that can truly help you grow will pass right by you.

The person getting in our way the most may very well be ourselves. Especially as a young person, when you start something new for the first time, you will inevitably face many obstacles.

There were so many challenges that I went through myself in writing this book. At least once a week, I constantly thought about stopping.

"Did I even have anything worthwhile to say? Would there even be anyone who would read this book?"

Such thoughts frequently haunted me, dancing around the recesses of my mind like a carousel of agony.

When I began university in the fall of 2020, I would find myself at three in the morning, finally having completed all my schoolwork for the day and desperately trying to work toward this book. The ubiquitous "imposter syndrome" would then rear its cruel head, as I would continuously find ways to critique my writing and compare my work to other literature. After every comparison, I would come out with a disheartening result. No one else is doing what I am doing, so is it me who's in over my head?

Young people tend to discredit themselves. We question our skills and knowledge while downplaying the value of our perspectives. However, I've found through personal experience that this is one of the greatest forms of self-sabotage.

Everyone has a unique perspective. It's useless to compare yourself with others as the content of everyone's work is so unique to themselves, and no less valuable in any way.

It wasn't me who was doing something wrong; rather, it was me who was going above-and-beyond.

I hope to touch those same young people who are also doing something that we might rarely see. To those feeling like they're alone. If I may, this is my Public Service Announcement: You're doing great. You're going above-and-beyond, and I do not doubt that whatever experience you're putting your effort into will help you achieve success in your own way.

As editor in chief of *Entrepreneur Magazine* Jason Feifer says, "Opportunities will not come to you. You have to go to them." While many of us may question what to do or even how to start, Jason reassures that even adults and professional entrepreneurs feel the same way.[208] Accordingly, the only way to grow despite the fear is to fight against it.

Through this chapter, I hope to inspire you with the stories of young people who also had humble beginnings but went above-and-beyond despite their age. I hope that you will find some of the teachings for this chapter to be useful in inspiring a project of your own.

We have more power than we think. And don't just take my word for it. This same mindset is echoed by many great leaders who started their journey of impact from a young age.

THE POWER AND POTENTIAL IN YOUTH

Ilona Dougherty is an award-winning social innovator and advocate for maximizing the value of youth in business, government, and civil society. Named as an Ashoka Fellow in 2009, Ilona's dedication to her passion has been recognized through her title as one of the Top 100 Most Powerful Women in Canada by the Women's Executive Network in 2015.[209]

Notably, Ilona is the managing director of the Youth and Innovation Project, a research project based in Waterloo University that seeks to better understand the role of adolescents aged fifteen to twenty-five in society. It consists of a vast literature review of the latest research in neuroscience and developmental psychology to understand the workings of young people's brain development. The research then makes

---

208 Jason Feifer, interview by Eric Koester, *Creator Series*, Oct. 5, 2020.

209 "Ilona Dougherty," University of Waterloo, accessed Jul. 13, 2020.

conclusions about what young people have to uniquely contribute to society during that time of their lives. Using these findings, Ilona offers consulting advice to support business and government in understanding how they can tap into the unique abilities of young people through intergenerational collaboration.[210]

Referring back to the "Inspiration" concept of Everyday Impact, Ilona's work is motivated by the experiences she went through herself as a young person that drove her to appreciate the value of empowering youth.

Ilona was, in her words, a "rural Canadian kid" who grew up in a small town in northern Saskatchewan. From her parents' influence, Ilona was always encouraged to let her voice be heard. At around fourteen years of age, Ilona gravitated toward environmental issues, getting involved in an organization at her high school that focused on environmental advocacy. Interestingly, the club was asked one year to babysit for an environmental conference that was happening locally, and at the end of the event, they invited all of the kids to come up for the annual general meeting. It was this opportunity that helped shape Ilona's future forever.

At that meeting, they asked if anybody wanted to put their name forward to be on the board of directors of this environmental organization. In a sea of apprehensive faces, one determined hand shot above the crowd.

---

210 "Youth & Innovation Project," University of Waterloo, accessed Jul. 13, 2020.

"I put my hand up," Ilona stated.

While Ilona was originally there simply to take care of the kids at this conference, her initiative allowed her to get on the board of directors. Soon after, the organization sent her to a national conference where she met Dr. Amelia Clarke, who currently works with Ilona now on the Youth and Innovation Project.

"I was walking down the hallway on the first night of the conference being like 'what am I doing here,'" Ilona described. However, she soon came across Dr. Clarke, who reached out a welcoming hand and invited her for a chat. That outstretched hand made a world of difference. Ilona felt empowered by how Dr. Clarke saw leadership potential in her and gave her an opportunity to voice her thoughts. This marked the beginning of a lifelong quest of impact to ensure that others would have their voices heard.

At fourteen, Ilona engaged in national public policy work around environmental issues, advising ministers of the environment on a federal level. When she was seventeen, she went to the United Nations Conference and contributed to changing the UN agreement to ensure that it contained a commitment to youth engagement. When she was twenty-three, Ilona founded the organization Apathy is Boring, a youth-led non-partisan charitable organization supporting the education of youth in democracy and encouraging them to vote.

***

Recalling her admirable beginnings, Ilona explained that three things led her down her path.

"One, I was very fortunate to have people in my life who always encourage me to speak my mind."

Ilona was by no means a one-woman army, and the support she received from her family and friends was valuable in pushing her forward.

"The second thing is that I was brave enough to put my hand up at this conference and say, 'Hey, I should be on your board of directors.'"

Ilona was not handed the opportunities allowing her to create impact. She started small, in an organization at her high school and forged new paths for herself through her initiative to ensure her own success.

"And the third thing is that I was fortunate to find a mentor who supported me and believed in what I had to offer."

Despite her juvenile age, Dr. Clarke saw the potential within Ilona to do more and helped cultivate that spark within her. While it may have seemed to Dr. Clarke like a simple gesture, to Ilona this was someone taking the time to engage with a scared fourteen-year-old kid. Dr. Clarke showed her that she had the potential to make an impact and saw something that many in her hometown had dismissed: a diamond in the rough.

***

Since then, Ilona has gone on to work with thousands of youths across Canada, delivering keynotes and TedTalks on the importance of youth empowerment. At the University of Waterloo, Ilona is the co-creator and managing director of the Youth & Innovation Project. In 2017, she gave a Ted Talk called "Wired for Innovation" at TEDxUW where she shared her story and research about the potential of youth in creating impact.[211]

Referring to the climate of the 2020 pandemic, Ilona noted that we're in a moment of rapid change carrying a complexity unlike any of us have seen in our lifetimes. "We are facing all sorts of problems that we're going to need to collectively solve. If we don't figure out how to meaningfully engage young people, I don't think we're going to be able to solve those problems." Proven through her empirical research, Ilona believes that the age of adolescence is the height of creativity. Willing to take risks, youth are set up to generate bold solutions to complex issues.

But the problem is that young people often lack the resources to scale and implement their solutions. "It's essential for innovation that we put young people with bold ideas together with folks who can scale and implement those ideas."

To tackle this challenge, Ilona provided certain key recommendations for how organizations can tap into youth innovation. First, she emphasizes the importance of prioritizing intergenerational collaboration. It's a matter of

---

211 *TEDx Talks,* "Wired for Innovation | Ilona Dougherty | TEDxUW," May 11, 2017, Video, 17:59.

thinking reflecting on whether the young interns in your organizations have opportunities to share their ideas with the decision-makers. Consider how you can create more opportunities to hear what unique ideas they have to offer. This can take the form of a reverse mentorship method where a young person is mentoring someone older or giving young people a position on the board of directors. The message overall is to ensure that there are opportunities for older professionals to learn from young people, thereby facilitating points of intergenerational collaboration.

Ilona does acknowledge that it is in human nature to feel apprehension toward change, and since young people embody new ways of doing things, it can be uncomfortable.

"So I encourage decision-makers to sit with that discomfort and still really listen to young people. Recognize that when you feel uncomfortable when someone presents you with a new idea, it's probably because that's when innovation is happening."

Ilona has accomplished many things, but the way that she found the opportunities to make that impact is one that anyone and everyone should follow. As a young person, it is more important than ever to set yourself up for success. Strive to do more than what's expected of you, as we also have a responsibility to work toward shaping the world we will soon inherit.

We are in a unique position to make meaningful changes in what we set our minds to. As Ilona's research found, there is great evidence of the traits that adolescents possess corresponds with the traits of successful innovators. The study claims that adolescents are "collaborative, creative, observant, curious, willing to experiment, willing to challenge the status quo, risk-takers, action-oriented and visionary."[212]

While it may seem daunting or unnatural, that first step will prepare you for a lifetime of impact. Believe in your own abilities, and simply by seeking new opportunities, you'll see a world of potential unfold, a whole path of impact along the crossroads of life that you never noticed before.

EMBARKING ON A YOUNG JOURNEY OF IMPACT
One might think this sounds fine on paper, but how does one begin? Where does one start?

Often, the best way to define our paths is to consider what steps that those similar to us have taken. The following stories will present other young individuals and their impactful experiences to offer guidance on how you can begin an early journey of impact.

---

212 Ilona Dougherty and Amelia Clarke, "Wired for Innovation: Valuing the Unique Innovation Abilities of Emerging Adults." *University of Waterloo Centre for Environment and Business,* (2018): 1-28.

COMBATING INEXPERIENCE AND THE POWER OF "DOING"

The best way to bridge the gap of inexperience is to seek those experiences yourself. Leo Xu, a student from the University of Western Ontario, exemplifies this "do-it-yourself" mentality. During the 2020 quarantine, Leo co-founded an organization providing educational opportunities and consulting partnerships for students around the world. But with his humanities-based background, no one would have guessed that Leo would be where he is now.

During high school, Leo was a self-proclaimed "social science" kid. He was an active community member, engaging in community volunteering and charitable causes. He was mostly active in civic engagement, having been involved in a plethora of activities, including student vote and working for his municipal government. In essence, everything Leo did before March 2020 had something to do with politics and civic engagement.

When Leo was in grade ten, he worked with an organization called the Federation of Canadian Secondary Students. They were one of the first groups to put forward a motion to the Ministry of Education to include financial literacy into the Ontario curriculum. Leo directly participated in this endeavor, and the experience showed him how the best way to grow is to do something that scares you.

"I realized that the best way to learn about your community, to develop the skills that you need—whether it's for school, jobs, or personal life—is by going out there and not being afraid to do the stuff that gets your heart pumping."

Now, Leo constantly reflects on the question of whether the things that he's doing make him uncomfortable. If they don't, he actively seeks out opportunities that will.

***

In the same way that COVID changed many people's lives, the pandemic was a catalyst for his entrance into a new path of life. In early 2020, it became clear that the educational scene was going to take a drastic fall. At the end of April, Leo came together with two of his friends to brainstorm how they could respond to the issue of the cancelled events, hackathons, and workshops. "How do we support student organizations to continue providing these resources for students whether they are incoming, whether they're prospective, whether they are not returning to school, whether they're on campus?" Leo asked himself. "How do we deliver that in a way that takes off the barriers between schools, to have this sharing of knowledge whilst fostering effective events?"

Yet Leo took it one step further by asking how to challenge these issues from an international perspective. This all stemmed from the fundamental realization that if the whole COVID-19 situation was hard for students like him even with the privileges that being in North America afforded, how would this be for students in Asia or Africa who faced existing disproportionate challenges to education that have now been exacerbated by the pandemic?

"In these times of changes, I am constantly reminded of those without access to education, sanitation, nutrition, or even basic rights. We cannot assign onus for everyone to make financial contributions. However, it is up to all of us to be reasonably informed and advocate with the means available to us," Leo explained.

What stands out about Leo's organization is that during this time when everyone is thinking about how COVID will impact *me*, how will *I* handle these circumstances, Leo and his friends were thinking about the struggles impacting other communities.

To address the dire need for educational resources, Leo co-founded Bridgespace, the world's first global campus community to offer virtual experiences and networking opportunities for university student societies. To foster engagement beyond their organization, Bridgespace provides resources including student networks and industry partnerships for students to host events for case competitions and hackathons, among others. Recently, they released an Impact Projects branch where they connect students with social ventures, charities, and startups to work on real consulting projects and solve real problems.

While Bridgespace has now built relationships with student organizations and universities around the world, the organization started small but progressed exponentially. The step of going from zero to ten backers is hard, as the Bridgespace team had to convince someone who had never heard about their organization to believe in and support their mission. Going from ten to thirty is a bit easier as you've got a small group of people supporting you. Then going from thirty to fifty is way easier as your network grows, and that small group begins to spread the word on their own. Generating that momentum took Leo's team a lot of time to gauge what people wanted and how they could respond to those needs.

The impact that Bridgespace brought upon himself and others has been life-changing. When it launched, Leo and his team released applications to the world through platforms like LinkedIn. "We had a breathtaking response that I did not anticipate. Something like two hundred fifty people applying to work with Bridgespace and none of this was paid, with over five hundred thousand engagements across our social media." And the range of responses came from an incredible international scale.

With pride, Leo recalled how he had an interview with someone from Azerbaijan who was going to the University of Pennsylvania. The student told him that he's been trying to get involved in youth leadership in his country, but the nature of his education system and government prevents him from gaining the same insight that organizations like Bridgespace are offering. In another instance, Leo received a message from a young man from Zambia who had difficulties making an account because the Wi-Fi was slow while he was herding goats during the day to support his family.

These two experiences showed Leo the things that he's taken for granted in university and validated what his organization was seeking to do; namely, to "bridge" the gap of access to educational resources in other countries. To date, Bridgespace has reached students from over one hundred countries. "There is that universal demand. At the end of the day, it's crazy to think about what students on the other side of the Atlantic are thinking and what they want to achieve."

Leo's story is indicative of the value of pushing your boundaries even from an early age regardless of prior experience. The potential for experimentation and growth is limitless, and the potential is even greater the earlier you start. You will encounter many opportunities offering valuable experiences, but for many, a presumed lack of experience is one of the main reasons why you might pass the opportunity. This leads to a perpetual cycle of stagnant growth, as declining such opportunities prevents one from gaining those background experiences in the first place.

It may thus be helpful to adopt the following mindset: to not seek opportunities for the sole sake of prestige, but rather to create an impact and develop oneself in an area of previous inexperience. Essentially, adopting a growth mindset and simply "doing" things is the best way to move forward.

As Leo advises,

"Whenever you ask yourself 'is this as far as I can take it?' it's usually never as far as you can take it."

It is in those moments more than ever that you must look around you, see who you can partner with, what kind of resources you haven't tapped into. And sometimes, just go for it.

HOW YOU GAIN WHEN YOU GIVE

After learning about the growth that comes from pursuing new opportunities, another young leader's path of impact demonstrates the value in young leadership and how we gain from giving to others.

Derek Nhieu is a community leader and Gates Scholar attending the University of Pennsylvania. He is the governor for the Pennsylvania chapter of Circle K International, the largest collegiate community service organization for college students.

To Derek, community service and altruistic actions reinforced to him the value of small actions. "I'm witnessing this, the power of one person because I think that sometimes people can get burnt out because they give so much, but they're not realizing that they're also receiving things." Oftentimes, those who may want to help may lose motivation as there always seems to be something that needs to be done. We tend to think that there's just so much that I can't do by myself. And this thought is disheartening.

But to this Derek described the parable of the starfish. The tale goes: There's a little boy on the beach who is throwing starfish into the ocean that have washed ashore. A man walks by and criticizes him, questioning whether he's even making a big difference. In response, the little boy picks up a starfish, throws it into the water, and says, "To that one I made a difference."

In essence, this encompasses the idea of "Everyday Impact;" how even the smallest of actions can be significant.

"I think about it a lot because sometimes we see people in the news; we see big philanthropists, we see big advocates and leaders and organizational leaders that are doing this massive impact. But what you don't realize is that changing one person's life is still very impactful. Your impact isn't immediately with the people you directly touch; it's a chain and legacy. After helping make one person's life better, hopefully, they can pay it forward and help someone else. And that's immediately within everyone's grasp."

Derek didn't raise an exorbitant amount of money for charity, but he did sit down with a middle schooler and walk him through what he could be when he grew up. In his view, even such simple conversations can play a crucial role in giving someone an "aha" moment, guiding them down a path of success. "And if he becomes a doctor or something, in a way I was involved with that and now he's helping all these other people. So the same way, it's just about the power of one and your impact and how that can multiply."

Derek refers to this phenomenon as the Power of One. "You don't have to be powerful, you don't have to have a lot of resources, you don't have to have a big network. All it takes is time and energy and your impact. Just ripples through all the people you've ever interacted with, and to me, that's something very powerful."

The act of giving, in his opinion, provides valuable potential for mutual benefit. For Derek, it takes the form of honing his interpersonal skills or simply promoting his character as someone to go to for guidance.

When asked about his most memorable memory of making an impact on others, Derek told a story of an encounter he received while teaching his workshop "Less Stress, More Success" which he has presented at numerous high schools. Derek explained that it serves as a mindset toolbox offering different strategies that the audience can use to build a happier, more productive life.

After he finished his workshop at a high school one year, a student walked up to him after the presentation and just started crying. While he was at first worried, the student told him that everything he talked about was something she needed to hear during the tough time she was enduring.

"I'm sure she still uses at least some of what I teach because at that moment I'm sure she remembered how I made her feel. And the same way she may not remember who I am, she might not remember what I did or talked about, but she remembered the way I made her feel, and in that way, I made an impact."

Life is not a zero-sum game. As Derek's story has shown, there is so much to receive through giving and helping others. "Just because you're helping someone else doesn't also mean you're not helping yourself or you're losing something," Derek confirmed. He believes that doing good for others will cultivate a massive positive impact that will overflow to help people be happier and friendlier. To create a world with less conflict, less division, and more collaboration. A world that everyone would truly benefit from. "The more people that work on the project actively, the better it's going to become. Everyone cognitively benefits."

AN EARLY START & A PASSIONATE CALLING

The theme of youth leadership and social impact is carried over to our final story about Alexa Grabelle, a sophomore at the University of Pennsylvania from New Jersey. What makes Alexa unique is how she defied the norm since the first year she hit double digits, epitomizing the value of starting early and connecting your passions to a need in society to create impact in the most meaningful way.

From a young age, Alexa was passionate about community service. She credits this to her family, who were similar in their desire to help others. The same values transferred over to her, and the idea of starting a service project was a goal of hers from a young age.

Early on, Alexa became attentive to a problem. Close to where she lived in New Jersey is Camden, one of the most impoverished cities in America. This community was just fifteen minutes away from her house. For Alexa, this meant she grew up in a community where there was relatively a lot more privilege than the people in Camden just next door. Alexa's religion teacher had also taught in a public elementary school in Camden, and from her teacher, Alexa learned about the dire need for resources in the Camden community.

Since childhood, Alexa has always been a very avid reader. She grew up surrounded by books, reading at a very young age. She understood their value, and upon realizing that certain schools don't have those same resources, felt a desire to do something.

With her interest in service projects, awareness of an exigent community need, and passion for books, Alexa united them into founding an organization called Bags of Books at just 10 years old.[213] It had humble beginnings as a small book drive for the community. "And I didn't have high expectations. I wanted to collect books for one class of students, so I was like, 'thirty students, five books apiece. Let me try to collect one hundred fifty books.' But within about two months, I collected two thousand books." Alexa recalled with a fond chuckle.

She was blown away by the potential for this initiative and has since grown it throughout middle school and high school. To date, Alexa's organization has collected over 160,000 children's books, which they've donated to students throughout the US and other countries. Bridging her passion for reading and need in the community, Alexa sought to simulate the Scholastic Book Fair experience in schools.

"What I always say when I'm talking to people who might want to start things of their own or just young people in general, is that it's important to find a way to connect your passions, to a community issue that needs a solution,"

---

213 "About," Bags of Books, accessed Jul. 15, 2020.

But Alexa's journey was not without its challenges. She describes how her age came into conflict with her endeavors, as adults in organizations she reached out to were shocked at her age. For Alexa, gaining their trust was a challenge. Looking back, Alexa considers this a part of her personal growth as running an organization allowed her to gain skills and experiences she wouldn't have gained anywhere else.

"I had to learn to face my fears and become more comfortable with showing people that kids can do things that are impactful."

When asked about notable success stories, Alexa made note of the teachers who expressed gratitude for her work. "Teachers would run up to me and hug me and tell me just how meaningful this project is for the students because I went to the same schools, year after year. So it ended up being this annual event that students looked forward to." Alexa recalled fondly. "We would play music, have all kinds of fun things like bookmark giveaways bags that were given out. It ended up just being this nice event that brought the community together." Alexa would receive thank-you note packages and stories from the children who received her books of how they ended up trading the books amongst themselves. Alexa was moved to see the genuine excitement that kids would have for their annual distribution event.

In the spirit of a young entrepreneur, Alexa had a fully motivated growth mindset that continued to see the potential for improvement. She went on to partner with Knowledge Is Power Program (KIPP) charter schools where she connected with one of the co-founders who then emailed all their district leaders to tell them about Alexa's organization.[214] This allowed Alexa to get responses from people in all different communities across the US who requested her help in distributing books.

"I remember just thinking back like that was a moment that made me realize that this is a national need not just in my community. And that led me to start trying to work with students and other locations." Alexa explained. As she recalls, one of the coolest things she's gotten to do through Bags of Books is starting an international convention for a youth group where she spoke in front of thousands about her organization. The students who attended brought their books from different countries and states, and through this national coming together of readers and changemakers, Alexa realized the potential of involving other teenagers to start their own branches of Bags of Books.

Alexa's experience has driven her to continue her pursuit of service in college. While she isn't sure of what she wants to do post-graduation, she is interested in education, writing, and social impact startups, most of which were tied with her Bags of Books experience. "But what I think is just the most valuable advice to give to a young person is to think about what your passions and skills are. Then you can always find something that aligns to that."

---

214 "About," KIPP, accessed Jul. 15, 2020.

TAKEAWAYS

Our current society is on a path of positive change and empowerment for the youth of today. However, just as Ilona stated, there is still so much more that we can do to tap into the maximum potential in youth.

Hopefully, these stories of young leaders will have relayed the message that age is not a factor against you, that the benefits of starting early far outweigh the false sense of security provided from starting later. In these young leaders' stories, while they're accomplishing great things, they all started in modest ways, whether that came from general volunteering or simple ideas that were spurred by a need. Be conscious of the difficulties affecting others and find a way to resolve them in a way that corresponds with their own passion, as your passions can be leveraged to boost your impact and motivations.

Everything still starts small—and in this case, young as well. Interestingly, common among all three student leaders is their possessed insights which mirror what seasoned professionals have said. From Leo's leap of faith and growth mindset, Derek's understanding of receiving through giving, to Alexa's manifestation of passion to action, it shows how you are not limited by your age but your experiences. If you don't seek out those experiences, you'll never get to where you want to go.

As the young generation comes of age, I urge us to take this time to ensure that the world we inherit is one that we already had a hand in creating. We should not enter adulthood with a sense of dread over the problems we need to solve; rather, it should be with excitement to enjoy the fruit of the labor we put in as youths.

Let us continue to shape the society that we want to see. Sow the seeds of our legacy from a young age and, in the process of bettering ourselves, create a path to continuous improvement.

PART IV

INNOVATION

CHAPTER 10

TAKING A LEAP OF FAITH

———

Everything beautiful that we create in life requires a leap of faith.

—PAUL BUDNITZ

The idea of the "leap of faith" is one of the most well-known idioms in the English language. Originating in the nineteenth century, Danish philosopher Søren Kierkegaard first used the term as a metaphor in his writing to describe the commitment to uncertainties such as the Christian God.[215]

Over the years, while the term still maintains strong connections with religion, it has more broadly been used to describe the decisions that one must make when faced with difficult choices. However, the idiom's meaning remains the same, telling us to challenge our apprehension and take a step into an exciting new reality. The initial struggle in taking that step, however, is significant.

---

215 "Leap of Faith," The Phrase Finder, accessed Jul. 10, 2020.

CHALLENGE VS. RECKLESSNESS

Sweaty palms. Whirring thoughts. Shaky breaths. The ubiquitous symptoms of anxiety and fear paired with the chilling sensation settling at the bottom of your stomach, freezing you in place. When we are faced with intimidating situations, our fight or flight symptoms kick in, and rightly so in the name of our self-preservation. But therein lies the common misconception of taking a "leap of faith." If these symptoms are meant to warn us of danger and steer us away from threats, why should we then willingly pursue something that scares us so?

A common misconception with "taking a leap of faith" is its comparison to recklessness and illogical thinking. A leap of faith is not one rooted in blind abandon; rather, it encompasses a belief in oneself and a desire for change. These leaps of faith don't involve diving into any risky, unknown situation that you know to be irrational. They reveal themselves when you are presented with something that seems uncomfortably different from what you usually do, but where you can't help but ask yourself, "what if?" It's when the thought of doing something new and different elicits a strong reaction of doubt yet accompanied by a unique contemplation and intrigue.

That is the difference between recklessness and challenging your comfort zone: that period of contemplation and knowing that the reward of engaging in such an action may very well be worth the jump, proving that taking a leap of faith is not simply throwing yourself blindly off a cliff.

In another analogy, imagine that you are at a crossroads, with three paths laid in front of you. One is the normal, inconspicuous road that maintains the same elevation and scenery. The second is a dark road filled with beasts, holes, and danger signs. The third is a shady path obscured by trees and fauna, but alive with the sounds of life and adventure. In this case, recklessness would entail the act of speeding down the dangerous second road. Taking a leap of faith, however, would be challenging your apprehension for the third path and seeking an unconventional but inevitably rewarding path of adventure.

As you will read in the story below, these rewards will often lead to amazing treasures.

SKYDIVING INTO INNOVATION

A cold sweat broke through his hairline as Jordan stood before the endless sky below him. The thought of jumping out of an airplane and free-falling like a shot-down bird terrified him. Be that as it may, this moment of fear would serve as one of the most defining moments of his life, and this act of jumping would set off a dramatic shift that would change his life forever, leading him down a path of innovation.

Our skydiving protagonist is Jordan Kilpatrick-Smith, a lifestyle development coach and founder of Thrive Health Solutions, a business helping clients achieve the life that they want to live. Since he was young, Jordan decided that he wanted to dedicate himself to making a positive difference on others, and his story of passion for service began through a humble story of standing up for others.

Jordan grew up in a small, predominantly Caucasian town of two thousand people. It was in grade five, Jordan recalls, that the first brown student in the school joined his class. "He's got a weird haircut," had been the class' thought at the time. The young boy was immediately outcast for his skin color, and the boy's father cried when the boy cut his hair in a desperate attempt to fit in.

One day, Jordan and his friends were playing tag in the school playground. His friends, however, would not allow the "different" child to participate. Witnessing this interaction, Jordan knew that it wasn't right. In an act of courage, he stood up and declared, "If he can't play, then I won't either." Jordan then went to sit with the new student, striking up a conversation. A friendship was quickly formed, and Jordan became the boy's first friend.

Shortly after, Jordan's friends came back and realized that they were wrong. "At that moment I saw what it's like to make an impact on people," Jordan recalled with a contented note. "And I knew deep down that that was the ultimate thing. If there's something to pursue, it's that."

With this value in mind, Jordan made it his goal to pursue a career that would allow him to make an impact on others. He always excelled in coaching and decided to become a lifestyle development coach for two main reasons.

Jordan first explains that he's always wanted to help people. When asked about what he wanted to do growing up, his answer had always been to help people, as nothing fulfills him more.

"One of the greatest feelings that I ever had was when you help someone, even if it's a small act of kindness; there's the old lady at the grocery store who's struggling to reach something so you help her out, or someone's walking up the stairs with bags of groceries and you offer to help carry it. It's these little things that just fill you with so much joy, so much satisfaction that it's like, why would I do anything else with my time."

For the second reason, Jordan explains that "there's a lot of suffering in the world that doesn't have to be. People get trapped in this rat race of anxiety and numbing, not knowing who they are. So, if I can help with that, well then, I think it's like my moral obligation to do so." While everyone faces their own daily struggles. Jordan wanted to use his skills to help people overcome those challenges.

Jordan's calling for purpose came in a particular event when he saw the suffering and need for change in the world. He was in his fourth year of university, working as a personal trainer. He was working with a particular individual who did everything that Jordan said to do, and Jordan did everything he was taught. But they didn't succeed. This turned out not to be an isolated incident, as Jordan quickly realized that there was something fundamentally missing from traditional approaches to health and wellness. It was experiences like this that led him down a path of considering how to view his coaching in an entirely new way.

What Jordan found to be the most difficult, however, was acting upon this problem regarding the traditional coaching style. "It was awful, in the sense that it was so filled with fear for me because we're taught our entire lives to fit in, we're taught to conform, to follow the rules we're taught to go with. While I thought that I was comfortable with the idea of stepping aside from that, actually doing it is a whole different story." This fear of acting upon his new ideas became Jordan's greatest enemy. The earlier challenges and experiences Jordan faced, according to him, all stem from a place of self-doubt.

"When I had an idea, it came with this implicit fear of not living up to what everyone else is expecting of you. And it makes it difficult to take action on performing that, especially when you don't have anything to show for it," Jordan explains. For him, it was a constant battle between wanting to quit and take the easy path to be willing to reach out and grab something that you've never touched before.

That all changed during his experience ten thousand feet in the air; his first experience skydiving with his first client.

Jordan's very first client was morbidly obese and severely depressed. While it seemed like no one could help her, Jordan decided to be the one to support her. In working together, one of the things that they realized was that she had a lack of passion in her life. "I guess I have to start doing things that I've not done before," she noted, "things I've wanted to do like a bucket list type thing and find something that I'm passionate about."

They ended up making a list of things that scared her, and one of them was jumping into a pool. So Jordan went to the local pool with her, and after a lot of coaxing and practice, they both jumped in. There was an initial euphoria, as they'd just done something that took her over fifty years to accomplish. Then she excitedly declared, "So next up, sky-diving!" Of course, Jordan reacted incredulously, dismissing the comment as a joke made in the heat of the moment.

So one can imagine his surprise when, just a few months later, Jordan gets a call from his client. "Hey! In June, I'm going skydiving," she announced. "And I want you to come with me."

Of course, Jordan's immediate reaction was the response *flight.* "Ah, you know, I just don't have money right now," he tried. As he recalled with a chuckle, he was simply listing off a litany of excuses for fear of tackling such a frightening activity. Yet despite his strong outward rejection of the idea, he was not all opposed to the idea. "As I was saying no, there's a voice inside of my head that was like Jordan. Stop being a b*tch. Come on," he explained. But skydiving had always been something that scared him more than anything else in life.

So when his client said she would pay for him, he realized that he was doomed. He told her to give him some time to think about it, and that he'd call her back. During this time of deliberation, Jordan remembers very clearly that one of the things that popped into his mind: "Would you rather live a life knowing you're held back by fear, or would you rather risk the potential of hitting the ground?" Jordan paused for emphasis, allowing me to soak in the quote while he relayed his memories.

"In other words, would I rather hold myself back and never achieve something because I was afraid of it? Or do you want to master your fear, right here, right now?"

As determination burned in his eyes, he recalled that "I said I would rather hit the ground than live another eighty years held back by fear."

He called his client back and agreed to go skydiving with her.

On doomsday, Jordan got in the plane and flew up into the air. Once they were high enough, it was time to jump. The solo divers went first and jumped instantly. As Jordan got to the edge of the plane, his mindset took on an interesting turn: "That edge of the plane represented fear for me. And I knew that on the other side of that door was everything I will ever want. And staying on the inside of the plane would be a life of everything I couldn't have." With that in mind, staying in the plane turned into something even scarier than jumping out.

As Jordan recalls, "It started this whole path for me: Now if something scares me or is uncomfortable, I know that I have to run toward it. Because that's where the pots of gold are, right? They're not at the end of the rainbow, they're like, in the middle of the pile of shit that you don't want to do."

Often when we think about overcoming fears, skydiving is one of the most popular ideas. But what makes Jordan's experience unique was the way that he made the experience out to be something so much more profound than doing it just for a bucket list or bragging rights.

It wasn't simply the act of squeezing your eyes shut, gritting your teeth, and jumping out of that plane. It was seeing this as a big step in his personal life, something that can help guide his future actions as well. While the act itself was a one-time experience, the profound personal transformation he went through is one that he continues to benefit from every day.

When Jordan comes across difficulties and challenges and things that spark an instinctual feeling of fear within him, he thinks back to his skydiving experience. "I cannot imagine anything scarier than that. It was an entirely irrational fear that had become so insurmountable that I thought I would never do it," he confessed. "But anytime I'm scared now, I say 'you jumped out of that plane. You can do this too.'"

Jordan began to respect himself and his ideas more, developing a newfound sense of freedom over his own choices. As Jordan explains, "If there's something I don't want to do, I don't do it now. Before, you can get pushed around as people will persuade you into doing things that go against your values or morals. [Now,] I am the one who makes the decision."

Finally, Jordan explains how taking leaps of faith have changed his self-confidence: "Confidence is a big one. And it's not that you're confident in the things you are. It's that you're confident in all the things you could be. It gives you the confidence to reach out and take those things because this whole journey that I've been down isn't about doing. It was a journey in 'becoming,' who am I becoming right now, and who I will be tomorrow."

Jordan carries that philosophy of taking the leap of faith to overcome fear in his daily life, and it led him to pursue his innovative approach to lifestyle development. As he notes, what's traditionally offered is the "I am the expert" approach where the "expert" will tell you what needs to happen so that you will go and do it. But these fitness plans are not sustainable since the trainer would essentially be living their life for them. As such, he realized that true change can only happen if the individual comes up with the idea and sees what's in their way themselves. "It's getting out of the mindset that I am the expert of your life. It's you [who] are the expert of your life. My job is just to help you see what's in the way."

Through his skydiving experience, Jordan was able to take that leap of faith into implementing this new approach and hosts discovery sessions with his clients where he asks a series of profound, meaningful questions which allow his clients to get to the root of their problems themselves and create the plan that works best for them.

"It impacted my life by giving me immense amounts of fulfilment and satisfaction and happiness. I get to wake up every day and say, 'what would make Jordan fulfilled today?' And I get to go do that." Jordan remarks with content. "I'm not driving a luxury car and I'm not living in a huge mansion, but I'm happy. And I think that's more than a lot of people can say."

Jordan had not only benefited in terms of his personal discovery. Indeed, the way that he applied that learning to create something wholly new was inspiring.

REFLECTION AND REROUTING YOUR PURPOSE

Jordan quite literally encompasses the philosophy of taking a "leap of faith." After hearing his story, I couldn't help but think of what might've happened had he found an excuse and not gone on that sky-diving trip. It forced me to consider my own experiences and how much I missed simply by saying "no" or trying to find excuses.

I reflected on my own regrets of missed opportunities: As a naturally more introverted child, I constantly refused opportunities to run for student government out of a fear of failure, only to hear disappointed sighs from my friends and even acquaintances who said they would've voted for me. I would shy away from engaging in public activities out of a fear of "embarrassing myself." The only embarrassing thing now is the fact that I let my fear get the better of me.

So for me, even writing this book was a major challenge. Rather than just a step out of my comfort zone, it was effectively an entire leap into something wholly new and stressful yet equally exciting. Sometimes one challenge can change your whole perspective, and it's so important not to let those opportunities slip by.

Other notable individuals share a similar story of risk and taking a leap of faith. A notable story comes from Suzanne Ma, co-founder of Routific, a company that reduces greenhouse gas emissions and waste by offering optimized transportation routes for businesses. Before starting her business, Ma had pursued a career in journalism and followed "all the right steps." After graduating at the top of her class from the Columbia University Graduate School of Journalism, Ma worked as a reporter for the Associated Press and DNAinfo. While she had achieved success in her journalism career, she felt unfulfilled.[216]

And so her leap of faith took the form of a ticket to the Chinese countryside and leaving her life in New York. There, she began to write a book, with circumstances she describes as "without a contract, without any connections in the publishing industry, without any guarantee that anyone but [her] parents would read and appreciate what [she] was writing."[217]

After she handed in her manuscript, Ma founded the startup Routific with her husband, a company that was soon featured on numerous headlines for its accredited route optimization software and contribution to helping companies cut carbon emissions.[218]

Ma faced numerous obstacles beyond technical challenges when founding her startup, most notably in the form of cautions from peers who warned against risking everything for such a risky dream. But despite those apprehensions, Ma overcame those fears and doubts and states that "like any fated relationship, if the timing is right, and if you have the skills, the determination and the resources to propel yourself forward, you can take that leap."[219]

---

216 Leah Arnold-Smeets, "4 Social Entrepreneurs Who Changed Careers and Changed the World," *PayScale Career News*, Jul. 29, 2016.

217 Ibid.

218 Ibid.

219 Ibid.

THE RISK AND REWARD OF ENTREPRENEURSHIP

Risks are often associated with the idea of entrepreneurship. *Forbes* has reported on this concept of a "leap of faith" numerous times in their articles, notably in tandem with entrepreneurship. In these articles rests a common theme where people have pursued the unknown. They saw value in what lay beyond the cliff of risk and took the jump with faith in their personal strength.[220]

For these leaders, regret was worse than failure. Jill Griffin, a *Forbes* contributor, gives her own advice on taking a leap of faith. "Get to know yourself. Dream again. And as you do, be thankful that you live in a country where, once you know what you want to try, you can actually take concrete steps toward it and eventually be whatever you want to be."[221]

However, social entrepreneurship and social impact can at times prove to incite a greater innate reaction of apprehension. Social entrepreneurs must constantly challenge the status quo to come up with ways of addressing the major social issues of our time and the conventional belief of businesses and jobs having the main motivation of one's self-interest. Rather than using innovation as a competitive advantage, innovation in social enterprises is driven by the goal of increasing public value by achieving improvements in governance efficiencies and service delivery.[222] Accordingly, social

---

220 Ian Hall, "Are You an Entrepreneur? The Leap of Faith," *Forbes*, Jun. 4, 2012.

221 Ibid.

222 Mark H. Moore, *Creating Public Value: Strategic Management in Government* (Cambridge: Harvard University Press, 1997), 1-402.

entrepreneurs must understand their society in the sense of what change is needed and how that change will occur. As the Social Enterprise Coalition claimed, social enterprise is an "inherently innovative business model."

That pressure and motivation are not insignificant, but just as we remarked at the beginning of this chapter, the reward can also be extraordinary. Successful social entrepreneurs can develop new approaches and improve upon old processes not only to benefit themselves through profit but change the lives of others for the better.

TAKEAWAYS

For anyone with remaining reservations, I would remind you to consider the concept of "Everyday Impact." Remind yourself that the greatest developments have humble beginnings, and the small things can compound over time to create a greater impact in the future.

Innovation can often be an uphill climb. However, the principles of Everyday Impact should help make it more manageable. The only thing left is to make the leap of faith to get to that hill in the first place. Seek first to know yourself, then to trust in your capabilities. The greatest returns come with the greatest risk, and those outward pursuits of potential can translate to great inward progress of your character.

As for Jordan's story? It reminds us that true innovation and change can be achieved by anyone, and to pursue it—even if it lies at the bottom of a ten-thousand-foot drop.

"For people who are reading this and want to make social impact, understanding our fear is probably the single greatest thing we can do to start down that path. Don't shy away from it. It is guiding you where you need to go."

CHAPTER 11

CHALLENGING
THE CONVENTIONAL

There is only one thing stronger than all the armies of the world: and that is an idea whose time has come.

—VICTOR HUGO[223]

THE IMPORTANCE OF DIFFERENTIATION AND OUT OF THE BOX THINKING

Today, we can't go anywhere without our mobile phones. But what people often don't know is that the treasured iPhone was not initially well received. People believed that a device without a physical keyboard simply would not succeed.[224]

---

223 "30 Of Our Favorite Quotes on Innovation," Workspace Digital, accessed Oct. 8, 2020.

224 Robert Safian, "Why Apple is the World's Most Innovative Company," *Fast Company*, Feb. 21, 2018.

While we associate safety with familiarity, the best way to unlock the door of progress is through the key to innovation. Our current society was built up from a result of constant progress facilitated through new ways of thinking and doing.

However, the idea of creating something can be intimidating. As the previous chapter noted, taking that leap of faith requires significant personal courage that is not often natural. This silent killer of progress is the idea that innovation entails the need to "reinvent the wheel." Our first thought drifts to technological breakthroughs like virtual reality or the founding of a charitable organization boasting a novel system. While it's important to think "outside the box," once again, this "go-big-or-go-home" mentality can serve as an obstacle to growth.

In the same way as the concept of Everyday Impact, I offer another perspective.

As *Forbes* notes, innovation is simply the act of introducing something novel or different. This broad definition in itself is comparable to the idea of social impact as it holds little constraint. In other words, similar to the idea that social impact can be achieved through small actions, even the small changes in an existing process can be innovative and meaningful. The current ideas we consider revolutionary came from humble beginnings. It was only through innovators who built upon each other's ideas that this continuous line of progress was created.

Innovators are not chosen by some higher being, nor are they born with minds naturally beyond our comprehension.

Rather, what remains consistent is their ability to consider other approaches based on what they already know. Coupled with a genuine passion and a tenacious drive for impact, anyone can be an innovator.

This chapter will offer the story of leaders who augmented their impact by delivering the services they were passionate about in a new way. You'll find that none of them re-invented the wheel; rather, they made use of accessible resources and prior knowledge to go above-and-beyond in taking their passion for action.

I hope that you will find inspiration in these ideas and build upon them yourself to open new doors for impact. So to begin, I offer an interesting story of a designer who found belonging in the unordinary.

EMBRACING DIFFERENCE & DESIGNING FOR IMPACT

Should you go with the flow and fit in with the normal or pursue the unconventional? While many may find solace in normalcy, innovation is only created through embracing our differences and leveraging that to create new things. My interview with Carlos Herrera would inform my understanding of innovation and how one can carve out their own "fit."

Carlos is an architect by trade and the founder of the brand "By Carlos Herrera," where he covers every aspect of design, including architecture, car design, art, and jewelry. He is a polymath, otherwise known as someone with many talents who excels in each and identifies himself as a multidisciplinary designer.

However, his diverse skills and unique character forced him to face many challenges in terms of fitting in. He always felt different from other children during his childhood, and upon entering the workforce, he experienced challenges with companies that didn't appreciate people going outside of what they asked. For Carlos, who always tried to think ahead and see anticipate problems that the company might have had, he found it difficult to stick with these rigid organizations that didn't appreciate employee input.

Before he discovered what a polymath was and identified himself as such, Carlos fell into a depressive state as he felt that his unique ways of thinking prevented him from fitting in anywhere. However, rather than seeking to change himself to fit the norm, Carlos sought to find something that fit him.

Rather than pursuing a job in only one of his specialized fields, Carlos created his own brand to allow his inner creative and innovative nature to shine. From that, Carlos didn't restrict himself and was able to create amazing designs that can help to create social good. "And to give more, I believe that the most important part is to understand myself."

Carlos designs for sustainable change. While you can certainly create a fancy car with aesthetic appeal, in his view, the most vital point of the design is the safety component. Accordingly, Carlos sought to design a car prioritizing the safety of the people inside.

One main design he implemented is to prevent parents from leaving their children and dogs in cars. It may seem trivial and too unlikely at first, but the terrible reality is that an average of thirty-nine children dies each year from being left in cars.[225] Thus, his idea was to implement an app in cars that notifies a parent if something alive is left inside. If there is no response, the app can contact the police. "To save lives, that is my main concern," Carlos explained. He strives to create the foundation for the architecture of the future and is currently focusing on green energy to create a vision for generations to come.

Now, Carlos continues to create designs that can better our daily lives and strives to help other creators embrace their difference and unique traits. "When I understood the real meaning of who I am, I embarked on a journey to help somebody else who is in a similar situation that I was. Part of my mission to help individuals, to say 'hey, you are not alone,'" he explains.

Carlos believes that there's so much more to life than only receiving. He wishes to leave a legacy by being a good role model to his daughter, inspiring her to pursue impact in her life as well. Rather than trying and make planets like Mars habitable, he is focused on using design to make the earth a better place. "My journey is to use my own identity and help other individuals to understand that is not a crime to say that you are gifted."

---

225 "Hot Car Deaths," Injury Facts, accessed Oct. 22, 2020.

THE ROOT WORD OF IMPACT & INNOVATION

There are many social issues prevalent in our world. Innovation offers the best way to tackle problems, presenting new ways to make an impact and paving the path for others. Such a notion is represented in the story of Eliana Trinaistic, a social impact manager at MCIS Solutions, a nonprofit organization dedicated to language advocacy. For Eliana and her organization, their innovation came in the form of using a new way to tackle social issues: through language advocacy.

Eliana began as an immigrant to Canada in 1993. She began by working in the health sector but quickly returned to school to pursue her interests. While pursuing a combined degree in environmental sciences and knowledge management, she soon learned that she didn't want to work in libraries or knowledge management institutions. As she reflected on her passions, Eliana realized that she was more of an activist and wanted to work in NGOs to understand the workings of a nonprofit.

In 2014, she became the executive assistant to MCIS Solutions, a nonprofit social enterprise dedicated to language advocacy and facilitating communication on a global basis. They seek to connect people through language, building authentic bridges that will break down silos between people and languages. The organization offers many language services including interpretation, translation, and training development in over three hundred languages.

During this time, social impact was a developing industry in Europe. This occurred after a big financial crisis where organizations realized that they had to start measuring their impact in ways outside of pure financials. In the UK, the Social Value Act of 2012 was passed and received Royal Assent, holding that every private or social organization had to manifest their social impact when they get government grants. This meant that it was not only essential to deliver on the grants' deliverables, but also to prove your positive impact on the community.

With this new requirement, Eliana went to her organization with an idea. She asked if she could integrate a social impact-focused aspect to MCIS Solutions to expand their dedication to positive change. Despite the then novelty of social impact management, her request was accepted. Eliana became the first-ever social impact manager in Canada with the official title in 2015.

She went on to help create a social benefit impact fund, where half of the fund was dedicated to services such as free subtitle translations for videos, and the other half to research and development. Eliana's role was at the intersection of research and development, with an emphasis on internalized, collaborative processes to facilitate projects.

"This is important because if you want to create change, you have to start from the bottom up. It's not a memorandum, it's not the decision of the board. You need this buy-in, at the base level."

Eliana refers to this as "intrapreneurship," the idea that changemakers should not just be focused on the impact they create for others but also act as agents of change within the organization itself.

Eliana also serves as a pro-bono coach for small social enterprises and remarks that "some people think they have to change the job but is not the job change that you need; If you want meaningful work, it's a matter of defining what you need and *recreating* your job. Think of the pieces and then build these pieces yourself into the job description." For Eliana, it is not a matter of fitting people into roles but designing roles around your people. It's making the best use of your intellectual capital and creating social impact within your organization to allow your team to flourish.

Notably, Eliana's story of innovation lies in the innovative ways that she tackles social issues through language advocacy. I felt a personal connection to this, as being an avid debater and a daughter to a family of immigrants, language is something I greatly value. Language can not only be powerful in general persuasion, but it has major implications in all other aspects of daily life.

A language barrier can be a terrible issue, as an inability to read an important document, for example, can result in numerous problems. Eliana has learned through her work with MCIS Solutions that language stands as the overlooked root of many problems including environmental issues. In Canada, the areas where environmental devastation happens most often involve indigenous communities. In those cases, a language gap can be the main factor behind conflict and miscommunications in using the land. For Eliana, language advocacy can be a backdoor policy into environmental rights.

The importance of language has been made even more apparent by COVID-19 which exacerbated the disparate issues caused by language barriers. "We can witness how many people are affected by an inability to simply read a document, and maybe not keeping themselves safe because they cannot translate the critical information that the health officials are offering," Eliana explains. Accordingly, she believes that support for the less conventional but increasingly important solution of language advocacy is more relevant than ever.

Languages facilitate global trade, exchanges, and relations. According to an article from Denice and Lawrence Welch on "The Importance of Language in International Knowledge Transfer," language can often be considered an integral component of corporate identity enabling the transmission and sharing of knowledge.[226] For purpose-driven organizations seeking to expand internationally, language support services can be a key factor in facilitating their impact.

It is even crucial for other fields like health care. For example, a notable study on the importance of language and culture in pediatric care presented harrowing results. Owing to the lack of an interpreter during pediatric emergencies, the results included misdiagnosis and severe medical failures for the children who weren't able to receive the proper care.[227]

Personally, it was quite surprising to see just how many issues can be caused by something that we take for granted every

---

226 Denice E. Welch and Lawrence S. Welch, "The Importance of Language in International Knowledge Transfer," *Management International Review* 48, no. 3 (May 2008): 339-360.

227 Glenn Flores et al., "The Importance of Language and Culture in Pediatric Care: Case Studies from the Latino Community," *The Journal of Pediatrics* 137, no. 6 (2013): 842-848.

day. Accordingly, the work of Eliana and MCIS Solutions should not be undervalued. Language lies at the root of many social issues and everyday problems. As such, Eliana seeks to create positive change through a language lens, thereby generating social impact in her own innovative way.

PIVOTING FROM HARDSHIP TO INNOVATION

What happens when everything you knew is forcefully ripped away from you? When COVID-19 struck, this was the narrative for business owners. But it was in the face of such troubling times that registered physiotherapist Dinah Hampson showed the resilience and innovative mind that made up her identity as an entrepreneur.

In the fall of 2018, registered physiotherapist Dinah Hampson co-founded Pivot Dancer, an online platform offering physiotherapy services and collaborative expert conversations in dance. Dinah also owns Pivot Sport Medicine and Orthopedics, a clinic embodying all the positive aspects of health care for people seeking injury recovery and optimal health.

As a physiotherapist, Dinah's career has been focused on bettering the lives of others. She loves the connections that she can create with her clients through their physical therapy sessions and helping them heal. Imbuing her passion in her work, Dinah was successful in her job.

But sometimes, life can hit us in the most unprecedented ways. This took the shape of the infamous coronavirus pandemic. According to studies conducted by the World Economic Forum, numerous businesses were forced to pivot to meet needs for their goods or services, and as financial resources depleted, over 40 percent of new ventures were projected to fall into a "red zone" where they had cash to sustain normal operations for only three months or less.[228]

For Dinah, being a physiotherapist during COVID-19 was disastrous because the norms were completely broken. Since physio is built on close contact, Dinah was forced to adjust to a whole new set of rules regarding social interaction. When quarantine shut businesses down, Dinah was suddenly faced with the burden of losing her regular income, forced to figure out how to continue her business in a way that she never had before.

With the problems of social distancing and quarantine that the pandemic brought about, all of the traffic and attention was moved to the online realm. But the greatest hurdle for Dinah during these trying times was using technology as she was never schooled in using it. She initially floundered trying to navigate the seemingly endless resources that the internet offered. Of course, Dinah has always used the internet, but before COVID-19, she's never looked at it as such an applicable tool to genuinely create connections.

Despite the marvels of her discoveries in this online world, the demons that the pandemic brought upon Dinah's personal life became increasingly prevalent. How was she to do her job when physiotherapy relies on physical contact? "How can I possibly use a remote tool where I'll never actually see

228 JF Gauthier, Marc Penzel, and Arnobio Morelix, "This is What COVID-19 Did to Start-ups in China," *World Economic Forum*, May 7, 2020.

that person in physical form? How do I create an authentic, meaningful connection?" She asked herself. How could she adapt to continue serving others in her work?

Near the beginning of the quarantine, Dinah received a call from a seventy-year-old lady named Dolly who called her in a panic. To preface, she had for years debated getting a knee replacement, and finally got the courage to have her knee replaced. The irony? Her surgery occurred right before COVID.

"I've decided to have this surgery, and now I can't do my physio," Dolly exclaimed.

Dinah, sympathetic to her plight, wished to help Dolly overcome these circumstances. Having heard of this emerging concept of online physiotherapy, she responded to Dolly by recommending that they both try this "online video thing." Dinah decided to embrace the intimidating online world, essentially throwing herself into the fire yet driven with a passion for change.

Dolly became her very first online patient. While the experience was new for them, it turned out to be more comfortable for Dolly than typical physiotherapy sessions as she didn't have to leave her house. She didn't have to worry about parking, and she learned how to use the technology.

Dinah would get together with Dolly three times a week and make her do exercises for her knee, teaching her how to massage her scars for pain and leg for swelling. For Dinah, it was amazing just how much she could see over the video and how much she could direct Dolly to do these exercises; essentially, making her hands be Dinah's hands.

They began their sessions in the middle of March, and when Dinah reopened her clinic on June 1st, Dolly came to see her personally. In two and a half months, Dolly had made a full recovery and could walk perfectly with no swelling and no pain. Even her surgeon was blown away, saying "I have no idea who you've been working with, but thank them because you're perfect!"

Beyond Dolly's transformation, Dinah reveled in her own journey of personal growth. From a background of no prior online physiotherapy experience, in just a few months, she was able to change someone's life while going through life-changing realizations herself that grew her business and character exponentially.

The sense of fulfilment that Dinah gained from helping Dolly was also augmented because of the hardships she had to overcome. Dinah feels validated in her impact; despite the method being outside of her box, she took it into her own hands to make it successful. "I can actually meet people this way and form a genuine authentic connection," she had relayed enthusiastically. To her, the COVID-19 situation also helped her expand her bounds within Pivot Dancer as well, proving that it was possible to create a meaningful platform for people to use everywhere that didn't require bricks and mortar.

Dinah then took online courses that helped her change the ways she used social media. She embraced video editing and graphic design apps that helped make her content more engaging to the audience to catch people's attention. She edited videos and tips for relieving pain and helpful stretches while doing online interview livestreams with professional dancers around the world to offer valuable advice.

While it may have been intimidating and wholly new at first, Dinah thought of her livestreams like a plate of hors d'oeuvres; Her ideas were the hors d'oeuvres, and if her viewers like the idea, they can take it. If they're not interested, they can let it pass them by. "It's a take-it-or-leave-it attitude. I'm simply focused on creating content, awareness, and community." She declared.

During livestreams, Dinah soon started to notice that a few familiar names would come regularly, so she started asking questions like "Where are you from?" and "What are you getting out of these talks?" to engage her audience. This helped Dinah bring exposure to her business in the online community while fostering trust from her followers. She produced valuable content and made herself available. "If people are tuning in regularly, then I've successfully created a connection and a community."

Dinah's journey was riddled with challenges and doubts. But she was motivated by a fundamental realization:

"Being in a negative space doesn't change anything. But if I do a live stream and someone gets something helpful from that, then I've changed something."

Even now, when Dinah feels herself getting in a bad position, she asks herself "What can I do that I can control? What can I do right now that's going to help other people?" She finds that conducting this self-reflection helps her focus her energy on something productive, evolutionary, and helpful.

Dinah now seeks to turn her learned experiences into a new normal. To sum up her innovative hurdle, Dinah explains that COVID-19 allowed her to "learn a whole new skill set that allows for the original skills to continue flourishing." She vows to continue keeping a strong online presence and loves that she can impact people outside of the four walls in which she works through her posts and live streams. Finding joy in doing simple things but which are helpful and impactful, Dinah furthers her own ripple effect of impact by providing advice for other entrepreneurs online.

"I just want to share more. And if I can create something really cool and different, awesome!"

What Dinah has gotten the most out of this experience is the resilience, strength, and benevolence that comes from choosing to be proactive in embracing innovation rather than succumbing to troubling external circumstances. Through her innovative journey of self-development and discovery, Dinah has reaffirmed the hallmark qualities of being an entrepreneur.

TAKEAWAYS

These stories, while all unique in their own right, show the different ways that positive change can be created through innovative methods. Whether it's embracing your differences like Carlos, looking at a problem in a different way like Eliana, or implementing different solutions like Dinah, innovation is the key to growth.

Don't let the conventional or the fear of novelty stop you; embrace difference and make your mark on creating positive change. It is only then that you'll open the door to a whole new realm of opportunity.

PART V

WHERE WE ARE NOW

CHAPTER 12

PUTTING IT ALL TOGETHER: THE MAGICAL MOVEMENT OF IMPACT

———

As a child, like any wide-eyed eight-year-old, I would start at the sight of street magicians and flock to their side. I would binge-watch videos of magicians on the *Britain's Got Talent* YouTube channel, getting my brother and jumping on the couch with our first-generation iPad.

While a magician never reveals their tricks, it's no secret that magic can attract nearly anyone's attention. This innate interest stems from our fascination with the unknown as we see acts so great that they defy our imagination. It's that moment of wonder and splendor when you think something can't be done but is then done in front of you.

Finding social impact, for me, has been like seeing a magic trick for the first time. Doing something for another person to potentially change their life for the better can be life-changing for oneself. That joy you see in someone's eyes when you do something for them never gets old. From a simple compliment to setting someone down a new path, the power of your actions can be nothing short of magical.

To me, this book-writing experience has been magical; not only allowing me to appreciate the value of my experiences but also in learning the incredible stories of changemakers in my own community. Seeing their eyes light up passionately for their work is a sight I won't soon forget. Notably, one of these very unforgettable stories is from the magician Dean Hankey who used entertainment to augment his impact and leave a lasting legacy.

PAY IT FORWARD AND PROFIT

A magician never reveals his tricks. But for this professional showroom magician, the secret to his craft is simply the act of giving. Dean Hankey is an experienced, veteran entertainer who performed over thirty thousand professional presentations for a wide range of audiences on how they could achieve success and create impact.[229] Yet the way that he promoted impact was quite unique to his industry.

Dean imbued his career with meaning by embodying the philosophy that you win by serving. Together with his magic

---

229 "The Pay It Forward and Profit Guy!" Dean Hankey, accessed July 10, 2020.

partner, Claude Haggerty, they raised over $20 million for organizations through fundraisers, tours, and live magic shows. Through his pay-it-forward-and-profit program, Dean generates value by teaching individuals and organizations how they can leverage service to achieve personal success.

"What we've done over our lifetime was done by simply asking and answering two questions: Who can I serve, and how can I serve." As a show business magician, Dean always included a leverage-able component of contribution in his business model. Rather than solely seeking payment for his services, he would request to have some other additional factor included that would allow him to contribute to the community in some way.

Dean's shows are known for leaving his audience with "aha" moments as highlights the true value of leveraging impact. However, he credits this ability to the great deal of aha moments that he has experienced himself in the past. Having partnered with individuals like Les Brown and Tony Robbins from the development industry, Dean learned a great deal about fulfilment and personal development.

"Because we're always looking for aha moments, we're always looking for opportunities to serve, for ways to encourage, serve, and help people get what they need."

Most importantly, Dean's background as a magician allowed him to create change in a unique way. Pivotal to the results that he achieves in others, Dean explained how he used the appeal of the entertainment industry to his purposeful advantage. "We leverage all kinds of tools and as a magician my entire job rested, rose, and fell on how well I engaged my audience." As Dean argues, nobody learns the art of engagement better than live entertainment professionals. Since engagement is so important to inciting action and results, Dean's career placed him in an exclusive position to generate impact.

In the same way that magic tricks can be forever engrained in your experience and memory, Dean explains that "The methodology of leveraging the principles of magic using simple yet profound ideas, using techniques and psychology to engage people can create an indelible first point of impact." It generates quick but long-lasting results, which stick with the audience for years to come.

Personally, this realization was quite remarkable as I was never fully conscious of the entertainment industry's potential to generate impact this way. Those skills from the entertainment industry are indeed valuable, allowing a transition from *show* business to *grow* business.

At the end of our meeting, Dean shared some insider tips about how service is valuable even from a strict business perspective: that you can generate more influence and income as a result of helping other people. In the world, there are more opportunities to give than to get. As he explains, there are more people who need help than there are people in a poised position to serve them. This means there are more opportunities for partnerships to make great things happen that might have never otherwise occurred had you been fixated on getting rather than giving.

"If you want to generate more results, and that means influence, impact, and income, then simply find ways to be of more value to more people. So stop selling, start serving, and serve your way to success."

Dean epitomizes the magic of giving. While the magic may be broken when magicians reveal their tricks, service is a gift that keeps on giving. Even when you begin to understand how things work, there are always new ways to define the industry and improve upon past methods.

In this very way, we can do to embody these same values in our everyday lives. By leveraging this magical potential in purpose-driven actions, we can create the same faces, reactions, and stories of awe from the people with whom we interact. So let us become the magicians of change to take actions that can inspire a generation of people.

***

Now as we near the end of this journey, I hope to encompass the magic of the journey thus far into a story that brings together the 3 I's of Meaningful Change. The following story is from Dean's magical partner Claude Haggerty, a renowned magician who raised over $4 million for charity while inspiring thousands of young students across North America. His story represents a culmination of all the 3 I's, showing how powerful these principles can be when you put it all together.

THE MAGIC OF EVERYDAY IMPACT

PRINCIPLE 1: THE GOLDEN TICKET OF "INSPIRATION"

The beginning of Claude's journey of impact emphasizes the importance of finding and pursuing one's inspiration. Claude started with humble beginnings, as most would never anticipate that a young fourteen-year-old kid with a stuttering issue would become a renowned magician who raised millions for charity.

Claude grew up in the small town of Kundan Ville, a farming community consisting of no more than eight thousand people. From a young age, Claude was a foster child who was passed on from family to family. Coupled with his stuttering issue, he lacked self-confidence early on.

School, to someone in Claude's vulnerable situation, was nothing short of terrifying. He would beg his teachers not to ask him questions in class for fear that his stutter would be mocked by the other kids. During recess, his bullies would mock his stuttering and get physical by pushing or tripping him. To escape the abuse, Claude would run to the library at recess and spend his time reading books, his personal haven. Little did he know that one fateful book would spark a series of events that would change his life forever.

On his second day in grade eight, when he went to the school library, he found a book on the table that someone had left behind. It described goal setting and having dreams, specifically recommending to write down one's biggest dreams on a piece of paper.

"At that time I was reading a lot of magic books. I used to get the magic books and learn a couple of tricks I could do with a deck of cards. So I write that I will build one of the largest magic shows in Canada. I write that I would have lions and tigers in my magic show. I write that I wanted to perform at an NHL Arena and raise a million dollars for charity."

Recalling this pivotal experience, Claude's eyes glazed over with bittersweet nostalgia. He then explained the second greatest event that set him down the course of his future. He took that paper and showed it to his principal.

As the principal held that simple scrap of paper containing such extraordinary dreams, he was taken aback and moved to fully support him. In an instant, a life-changing connection was formed.

The next day, Claude goes to his principal and performs a magic trick. The principal was amazed by the trick but proceeded to recommend something seemingly unfathomable: He told Claude to show that same trick to the boys in the schoolyard, the very people who'd been bullying him.

"They are going to love that trick," the principal assured him.

But Claude responded in terror, "No, they're gonna knock me down and jump on me and punch me and kick me!"

Seeing his scared opposition, the principal supplied that, "I'll tell you what. I will look out the window, and I'll make sure you are safe. If they get physical, I'll come right out. But they're gonna love this trick."

Claude seemed to contemplate this before simply looking at him and confessing, "I'm afraid."

The principal nodded, empathetic to his plight. But he gave a simple yet profound explanation that Claude remembers to this day.

"He said Babe Ruth had two world records," Claude retold. "Babe Ruth had the most home runs out of any player in the baseball league, hit the most home runs. However, Babe Ruth also had the record for the most strikeouts."

During our call, Claude looked at me and asked, "Do you know why he hit the most home runs?"

I responded with a contemplating, quizzical look, which prompted Claude to explain what his principal told him. "He said it was because he was not afraid to strike out."

With his principal's lesson in mind, Claude went up to his bullies during recess, shaking with fear. After showing them the trick, Claude ran back inside. But the bullies were left amazed and impressed.

His principal came to see him soon after and simply said, "I am so proud of you."

Two days later, his principal asked his homeroom teacher if Claude could be excused to meet with him. Claude was worried that he was in trouble, but when they reached the office, his principal held up five tickets to a big magic show in

Hamilton. In a slip of the mind, he explained that he bought five tickets, but there were only four people in his family.

"So here's what I did. I had a random draw from the seven hundred kids at the school. You win this free ticket," he announced.

Claude was taken aback, and quite elated. But he was not quite so naive. He knew there was no way this was just a coincidence, but what made this impactful was that the principal didn't say "You won this ticket because I feel sorry for you." He didn't say "You won this ticket because you don't fit in." He said "Anyone could have won this, but today was just your lucky day."

He sustained Claude's dignity, all while allowing him to take advantage of an incredible opportunity without embarrassment.

Two weeks later, Claude went with his principal to see the show. The performance was extravagant, featuring over-the-top lighting, equipment, and quality. Awestruck, during the show Claude tells his principal, "This is what I'm going to do one day."

The principal looked at him and said, "Yes you are."

Throughout the remainder of his high school experience, Claude continued to hone his skills and pursue his passion. In grade twelve, he performed an illusion he watched with his principal at that performance in front of his school's seven hundred students. For Claude, this stood as an early symbol of how far he'd already come.

On the last day of school, his principal was awarding seven awards of achievement that, as Claude explained, are usually reserved for the truly exceptional. Those Einsteins and Usain Bolts, the students with 99 percent averages and set records on a track team.

The first six students who received the awards of achievement all fell exactly in that category. But when it came time to present the last trophy, the principal called Claude to the stage. He gave him that trophy in front of the school to commemorate his journey of growth—of how far he'd come from a scared, stuttering kid in grade eight to a budding magician.

"I never forgot that." Claude paused, his voice shaky as the emotions flooded through him again. "And that became the cornerstone for my entire magic business for thirty-five years."

Claude found inspiration from his principal's kindness and began to think of ways he could pay it forward. When he became a professional magician, taking inspiration from his own experiences, he carried on that kindness by advocating for anti-bullying and helping children pursue their dreams just as his principal had done for him. Leveraging his past as a springboard for his purpose, Claude embarked on a journey of impact through magic.

PRINCIPLE 2: THE MAGIC IN PURSUING ACTIONS WITH "IMPACT"

Throughout his magic career, Claude not only delivered shows in major venues, but he also partnered with over eight thousand principals to bring his show to their school. This allowed Claude to talk to children about overcoming bullying, the importance of writing down their goals, and sharing those dreams with others.

"My principal bought me a $10 ticket. And I raised over $5 million for nonprofit groups after that."

When Claude partnered with these principals to do the event at their school, he would do a free show sprinkled with magic tricks but focused on talking about one's goals and self-confidence. But he would go above-and-beyond by arranging a subsequent evening performance in the community where the schools and local nonprofits would share in the revenue.

At every school, he would give two tickets to his show for every class. This meant that one boy and one girl in every class would win a magic ticket, just as Claude had from his principal, to attend his show, hear his story, and be inspired. "I helped over 100,000 children come to my show for free to be inspired by the ticket they won from their principal," he explained. "And I was able to generate millions of dollars in sponsorships to make that happen."

The magic of impact, however, didn't stop there. The stories of certain winning children were nothing short of magical.

***

As Claude was packing up in the parking lot after one of his shows at a school, a grade-one teacher approached him with tears streaming down her face.

"Mr. Haggerty, I gotta–I gotta tell you something!" she exclaimed in a tearful but joyous breath.

She explained how she had put the kids' names on pieces of paper, rolled them into a ball, and put them into a cup. She then placed a big X on the floor and stood on a chair above it. She then tipped over the cup, and whatever name remains closest to the X would get the ticket.

"And the most magical thing happened. One tiny piece of paper landed right on the center of that X." She remarked emotionally. "That little winner was the only foster kid in the class."

At this point in our interview, Claude paused to let the meaning of that experience sink in.

"We talk about the power that one person could have. And I think we as humans think about how we could be that one person who can make that kind of difference. 'I'm a stuttering foster kid with no confidence, how can I change the world? How can I make this a better place?'" Claude began.

"You look at people like Terry Fox, changing the world like a God," Claude confessed. But it's these profound, magical experiences that helped him realize that. "I think we all have the ability to help people."

Claude then recounted another one of the most memorable moments in his career. He was at a school, having just finished his program, and a little girl no older than nine was waiting to talk to him. She introduced herself as Emily.

She didn't talk at first, just stared at Claude. It was after Claude said hello that Emily opened her mouth, saying, "I-I-I-I-I stutter too." And as she said that she started crying.

Claude was taken by surprise but asked the teacher for a few minutes with Emily. He sat with her at the stage, taught her a simple card trick, and walked her back to class. After telling the teacher what they did, the teacher asked if Emily would be willing to perform that trick in front of her classmates. When she did with a little help from Claude to make sure she wouldn't stumble, she got a standing ovation from her class. Later on, Emily's parents came to Claude and thanked him, saying that they could see a difference in their little girl that day.

PRINCIPLE 3: THE MAGICAL SECRET OF "INNOVATION"
Such incredible experiences motivated Claude to pursue more unique, innovative methods to create impact through magic.

Claude began to host new magic workshops. He went back to the schools that he performed at before and had the principal pick one or two children from each class. Then, he would personally teach that child magic. "We taught each child to perform a jaw-dropping magic trick and that night, those twenty-five children put on a magic show that served as the fundraiser for the school. These twenty-five kids were the stars of the show," Claude explained. "Sponsors come out of the woodwork like crazy to help make that happen."

As Claude recalls, the shows produced not one dry eye. These children would come into his workshop with their heads down, but after the workshop, perform on stage flaunting jazz hands and beaming smiles. The following day, principals would write to Claude saying, "It's unbelievable. These kids are now walking down the hall with their head up, beaming ear to ear, and everybody's giving them the high-five for what they did last night." As each noted, they could see the difference in these children in just twenty-four hours.

***

To Claude, magic was a medium for making his difference in the world–it was something that he had and could use to create impact.

He also developed a program that helped him maximize sponsorships and impact. He would go to schools, do an evening show for the families in the community, and donate a portion of the ticket sales back to the school. He would even take $5 off the ticket price for those who purchased food items because it was all donated to local food banks. This way, he raised millions of pounds of food. In exchange for this free show, schools would help him promote his professional shows so Claude could earn more money to help the schools and food banks even more. And kids from organizations like Boys and Girls Clubs and Big Brothers Big Sisters would just get tickets for free to come.

"I got more than compensated by just giving this away because other people lined up to help me to make sure that I could continue to do this right. And I did this for thirty-six years."

Claude retired from show business in 2016 but now helps entertainers, coaches, and speakers leverage their talent in their story. Through his own experiences, Claude teaches others how to use their passion and skills to make a difference. "So this way, by helping one person, they could affect thousands more."

Just as others had inspired him in the past, Claude continues to dedicate his life to service. The trick up this magician's sleeve? To lead new generations of impact founded on people's passion and heart to serve.

TAKEAWAYS

Whether you're learning, engaging, or benefiting from the positive reverberations of social impact, you can be brought back to the sensation of being blown away by magic. In the same way that a simple trick can completely shape your beliefs, one act of positive social impact can leave a lasting impression and change one's life for the better.

In this way, like Dean and Claude, utilizing the *3 I's of Meaningful Change* can help us all become magicians of impact, allowing us to pursue actions that can inspire generations of future changemakers.

CONCLUSION

———

While the Impact Revolution shows greater and greater promise, there are still many with traditionally self-interested views. The preconceived idea of this "dog-eat-dog world" or the "go-big-or-go-home" mentality is still deeply entrenched and not easy to uproot.

On an individual basis, the common belief seems to share a similar self-interested view: It is in human nature to gravitate toward financial incentive, and you can sway altruism through monetary means. For many, they still believe that purpose and profit are exclusive, and people seeking to make a difference will be sacrificing their livelihood. Others are bystanders, those who subscribe to the notion and belief of social impact but make no actions to support it. These individuals are often misguided by the mistaken view that impact can only be created if you have financial wealth and a powerful position or that impact can only be created if you become a social entrepreneur or nonprofit manager.

These traditional views are self-sabotaging. By prescribing to theories like shareholder primacy, we would be neglecting the perfect opportunity to produce win-win situations through business.

The traditional economic idea that humans will naturally choose the action which will provide them the most financial incentive is also damaging, causing us to fail to consider the intangible benefits from creating positive social impact which can often be valued higher than a financial return.

The bystanders, while at first glance may not seem to be harming anyone, are indeed presenting a problem through their own inaction. Through their own self-doubt, they may see themselves as unable to make world-shaking change, disheartened by the philanthropic demonstrations of billionaires, and content to leave the work to others. In this way, we are losing a great deal of individuals who very well have the ability to shape their communities and overall society for the better.

WHY EVERYDAY IMPACT?

Realizing these gaps was a deeply concerning issue. Many groups I'd come across were still raised on those counterproductive traditional perspectives.

I feel compelled to bring others on this journey of impact exploration and discovery in order to help inspire young people to do more than just the status quo in their own future careers. Capitalizing on the current positive trend for sustainability and social impact, a book like this would be beneficial for young people and current professionals alike.

Resources on social impact are not often able to make a genuine connection to the majority, as they often cover only the biggest impact initiatives, causing everyday people to feel disconnected and unable to relate to such gargantuan contributions.

My young age is a beneficial factor in providing me with the ability to see the situation with a fresh pair of eyes. Being a part of the young generation who will inherit the future, I firmly believe in the transformative power within each of us to make a positive difference on both a macro– and micro-level to help shape the society that we want to see.

Social impact can be any action which affects the community around you, and I believe that positive social impact can and should be achieved by anyone. Rather than major one-time catalysts, I find strength in the progression and accumulation of numerous pieces to one whole. As my theory of Everyday Impact describes:

It is through the power of everyday actions and small contributions which have the ability to compound over time to create an even greater impact in the future. Everything starts small, and anyone can create change no matter who or where they are.

VALIDATING EVERYDAY IMPACT: A SHORT RECAP

In the beginning, I presented a brief history of social impact, describing the development of people and industries that got us to where we are now. Here social impact is defined as a dynamic and ever-evolving concept. With its relative novelty and broad definition, there is great potential for individual actors to implement social impact into other fields and redefine whole industries for the better.

We then explored the 3 I's of Meaningful Change, starting with the principle of Inspiration. Meant to help you find your own inspiration for impact, we determined how your previous struggles can serve as catalysts for change to drive your purpose in a meaningful way. We also explored the idea of Purpose over Profit and the greater value in having purpose motivate your actions rather than self-interested motivations. From this section, I hope those who may have gone through struggles in their own life can see ways that they can use those experiences to develop oneself and pursue purposeful actions.

The second principle of Impact emphasized ways that anyone could contribute. The notions of doing more for one's community, harnessing the power of kindness, engaging in meaningful discussions through advocacy, realizing the potential in business, and capitalizing on the potential for youth to create impact are all important ways in which people can engage to make a difference. From this section, I hope you will find ideas that you resonate with and implement them yourself to create a positive impact in the people around you.

The third principle of Innovation begins with the idea that true progress requires a leap of faith, validating the fear of exiting familiarity, yet empowering one toward the potential in the new. We then explored numerous principles and ways that one could use to inform their own innovative ideas, such as looking at the root of a problem and using challenges to inform new ways of doing. From this section, I hope you can use the stories given and build upon them to devise your own way of going above-and-beyond in for yourself and others.

***

Overall, the individual stories of impact described in my book validate its message. Even well-known individuals such as Muhammad Yunus and Claude Haggerty all began from humble beginnings, and out of nearly everyone I've interviewed, they all told a story of how they worked their way up. They all testified to the role of collaboration and coming together, accumulating to create a larger change consistent with my idea of the compounding effect of smaller actions. But what was most surprising is just how many treasures can be found in your own backyard. Even beyond the stories of those famous individuals I included the people I interviewed held nuggets of wisdom comparable to some of the greatest advice we hear from CEOs, motivational speakers, or the renowned individuals we know today.

THE PERSONAL IMPACT OF EVERYDAY IMPACT

I came into this book with a general understanding of social impact. I had a basic understanding of business ethics and social responsibility, and was more or less familiar with many of the different ways that people have created impact through their careers. However, this is miles away from the understanding I've now reached after going through this book-writing process.

In seeking to interview a variety of different people about the ways that they pursue impact, I was able to appreciate a contrasting phenomenon. I realized that although the details of the lives and jobs of people I've interviewed were different and unique to themselves, I found that so many of the methods and values that drove their decisions and thinking were extremely similar. From traits such as risk-taking to their own stories of humble beginnings, I've found that people seeking purpose and impact are unified by the traits noted in the 3 I's of Meaningful Change.

On a more personal and emotional level, unashamed to say, I've gotten emotionally invested in nearly all the interviews I've had. As I listened to the stories of each of my interviewees, the tales of their lives enraptured me in the same way as watching a movie or reading an autobiography. I shared their sadness as they recalled the difficult times of their life, and I reflected their smile as they told of their greatest accomplishments. It was a bonding experience unlike any other.

Through this process, I have made personal discoveries that have shaped my perspective of my society. I've come to fully realize and appreciate the fact that anyone has a million-dollar story, and if given the opportunity, nearly all people can provide a quote worthy of being inscribed on a plaque. From these stories I've compiled of real people no different than you and me, I have highlighted the power in anyone to make a meaningful, positive impact in the world.

Power and potential lie in each and every one of us; it's only a matter of letting it out.

***

Since I was a kid, the magical land of literature shaped my fondest memories. I was often enraptured in the magical lands of fiction or inspired by the invaluable tips and motivating advice from nonfiction.

Nearly every time I read a book, I would be flabbergasted by how perfect the story was told or how the words came together. I saw the author as this divine being, and while I possessed a profound respect for their work, I never thought of myself as capable or worthy of accomplishing a similar task.

Over the past year, this book-writing process has been nothing short of life-changing. As a first-time writer, I have come to understand the immense amount of work and care that goes into developing a long piece of writing that you can call your own.

Not only did the interviews, stories, and research I compiled teach me about the opportunities and ways to pursue meaning in life, but the kind feedback and comments I received from those I interviewed who supported me in my endeavor. As they voiced their admiration and respect for the project, it emphasized and verified the potential in any young person like me to do good and make grand impact. It has become a platform to provide voices to people that might otherwise not have the chance to share their stories and insights.

Similar to how an entrepreneurial venture can help to open so many new doors, writing the book has been one of the best decisions of my life as it has allowed me to develop my network and understanding of my greatest passion.

I've been able to meet so many amazing people who are really impact oriented and seeking to make a difference with that genuine passion and heart to serve. And that's just the most inspiring thing to see—that there really is potential in this. While allowing me to go on my own personal journey of discovery, this book has hopefully taken you, the reader, along on this same trip.

This book serves as the culmination of my impact. In writing the book itself, I have helped share the stories of people while inspiring them in my own way whether through inspiring them to write their own books or highlighting the potential in youth for positive change. With my fundamental goal of inspiring readers through these stories, I'm creating my own impact in a unique sort of way.

A PARTING BUT PURPOSEFUL CALL TO ACTION

Before you read through his book, what did you think of when you saw the words "Social Impact"?

The traditional idea would incite old images of NGOs and philanthropic checks from the top 1 percent.

This is essentially why I wrote this book. To show everyone a new perspective on this magical industry and to empower each and every one of its readers to recognize the potential within themselves to make a difference in the world, as social impact is not limited by any one industry or approach. It is the way by which you can make your mark and help shape our society into one that you and others would thrive in.

For those who've come this far, my greatest sense of fulfillment from this book would be for you to go out and apply the principles of the 3 *I's of Meaningful Change* in your own life. I will know that I have done my job if you have found motivation or inspiration from any of the stories I've shared, if I have provided you with a new perspective and interest in social impact.

While I have expressed insights for impact, no one is perfect. I simply try to strive to live by these principles and lessons to the best of my ability and set a good example for others. Even after reading this book, you should not expect yourself to come out a completely changed person; rather, I hope that you'll resonate with certain ideas and principles, feeling enlightened or excited to try out new, meaningful actions.

That is why it is called a *journey of impact*. This a continuous path of progress rather than an elevator to the top. If there's one thing this book emphasizes, it's the idea of small, consistent actions done over time which create a greater impact in the future. In the same way, it's in implementing small nuggets of the principles of Everyday Impact that you can start and continue down the path of meaningful change.

In the same way as how we began this journey, I implore you to once more strive to "Be the change you wish to see in the world."

Everyone can create positive impact; and I hope that you will create meaningful change in your own lives for yourself and others to share your *Everyday Impact* with the world.

ACKNOWLEDGEMENTS

———

This journey is not one that I have ventured alone. Indeed, I'd like to acknowledge the incredible people who have given this book the legs to move forward. First and foremost, to my wonderful Feng Family: Thank you for being my guiding inspiration and greatest support. I would not be here without your sacrifices, and I hope that I have done you proud.

Many have walked with me along this path of purpose. Here are the kind backers who have helped make this journey possible:

Nadine Maia-Lynn Bongers, Yan Chen, Isabella Milano Medina, Parsa Razeghi, Yu Gui, Tiffany Yau, Leigh Naturkach, YongZhong Zhao, Michael Huang, Jen Fraser, Emma-Rose Hoog, Nethu Vitharana, Marco Lu, Jordynn Bateman, Max Xu, Mary Long, Poonam Gawri, Danny Wu, Rishi Simha, Joe McMaster, Joanne Chu, Desiree Izecksohn, Emma Liang, Meara Lee Nordquist, Yihan Li, Megan MacEachern, Shyama Dave, Anastasia Mason, Maryam Milani, Nancy Liu, Zhu Jun, Michael Setrak, Roberta Harper, James French, Nora Chan, Brandon Nguyen, Victoria Boulus, Daniel Shen, Nina Peng,

Shawna Patruno, Cecile Blilious, Kelly Lorena Garcia-Ramos, Carlos Herrera, Ellie Petrak, Bing Zhong, Yu Min, Danny Khanna, Émilie Blondin, Ziyi Xiao, Peilin Qian, Eric Koester, Rosa Lokaisingh, Wei Ji, Muskan Nagra, Susan Bond, Stewart Leese, Jordan Kilpatrick-Smith, Angela Brown, Jinnie Yang, Efosa Obano, Tony Peng, Kiera Ballinger, Sarah Asfari, Dawn Vanier, Siming He, Lindsay Doke, Sonia Kurmey, Sui Chen, Carter Yacyshyn, Chenzhu Bai, Ilona Dougherty, Vincent Qin, Francois Lupien, Annie Hardock, Xidong Zhang, Eric Wang, Leo Xu, Amir Al Musawy, Kyle Hudson, Selina Zeng, Derek Nhieu, Carlos Garcia, Deborah Olatunji, Will Smith, Mark Walker, Brenda Marie Sheldrake, Dawn Truong, Cole Smith, Bert Maes

Thank you for believing in my book's message and being a part of my pre-sale community. It was only through your contributions that this book could come into fruition.

Lastly, I'd like to acknowledge all of my interviewees in this book:

A special expression of gratitude to my incredible interviewees:

Ahlam Nasser
Guillaume McMartin
Yan Chen
Barry Li
Rosa Lokaisingh
Efosa Obano
Brenda Marie Sheldrake
Jeff Perera
Leigh Naturkach

Tiffany Yau
Ilona Dougherty
Leo Xu
Derek Nhieu
Alexa Grabelle
Jordan Kilpatrick-Smith
Carlos Herrera
Eliana Trinaistic
Dinah Hampson
Dean Hankey
Claude Haggerty

Your stories make up the heart of the story.

I would like to acknowledge Eric Koester, Brian Bies, and the entire NDP team for allowing me to realize my authorship dream. To my MRE editor Bianca DaSilva and author mentor Kyra Dawkins, thank you both for being my pillars of support both in writing the book and dispelling my self-doubts.

As a young, first-time student author, I am beyond grateful to each and every one of you who've provided me with opportunities and guidance along the way. You are all a forever part of my journey of impact, and I hope that through this book, I have been a part of yours.

APPENDIX

———

INTRODUCTION

Alvarez, Simon. "Tesla Energy's Role in the Fight for a Sustainable Future Explained by Elon Musk." *Teslarati*, July 23, 2020. *https://www.teslarati.com/tesla-energy-master-plan-elon-musk/*.

Dahl, Roald. *Charlie and the Chocolate Factory*. New York: Alfred A. Knopf Inc, 1964.

Dictionary.com. Academic ed. s.v. "Third Eye." Accessed August 23, 2020. *https://www.dictionary.com/browse/third-eye*.

Genesis. "Be the Change." Accessed December 14, 2020. *https://www.genesisca.org/single-post/2019/06/17/be-the-change*.

Investopedia. "Dog Eat Dog." Accessed December 20, 2020. *www.investopedia.com/terms/d/dogeatdog.asp*.

Metcalf, Tom. "Jeff Bezos Donating US$10B Barely Dents his Surging Fortune." *Bloomberg News,* Feb. 18, 2020. *https://www.bnnbloomberg.ca/jeff-bezos-donating-10-billion-barely-dents-his-surging-fortune-1.1391945*.

Sinek, Simon. *Start with Why: How Great Leaders Inspire Everyone to Take Action.* New York: Portfolio, 2009.

TEDx Talks. "Ending Global Poverty: Let's think like Silicon Valley | Ann Mei Chang | TEDxMidAtlantic." Jan. 10, 2017. Video, 12:24. *https://www.youtube.com/watch?v=cgUho7hiZ34.*

The Journal of Student Science and Technology. "Online Research Coop Program." Accessed December 18, 2020. *https://journal.fsst.ca/jsst/index.php/jsst/pages/view/coop.*

Zhivago, Kristin. "Business Makes the World Go Round." *Kristin's Wisdom* (blog). Sept. 10, 2018. *https://kristinswisdom.com/business-makes-the-world-go-round/.*

CHAPTER 1: A BRIEF HISTORY OF SOCIAL IMPACT

All American Speakers. "Bill Drayton." Accessed Nov. 23, 2020. *https://www.allamericanspeakers.com/celebritytalentbios/Bill+Drayton/383862.*

Architects of Peace Foundation. "Bill Drayton." Accessed Nov. 23, 2020. *http://www.architectsofpeace.org/architects-of-peace/bill-drayton.*

Ashoka India. "Ashoka's History." Accessed Nov. 23, 2020. *https://www.ashoka.org/en/story/ashokas-history#:~:text=Beginning%20in%20India%20in%201981,for%20far%2Dreaching%20social%20change.&text=The%20Ashoka%20Fellowship%20became%20a,association%20of%20leading%20social%20entrepreneurs.*

Ashoka United States. "A Little Empathy Can Go a Long Way: The Bill Drayton Story." Accessed Nov. 23, 2020. *https://www.ashoka.org/en-us/story/little-empathy-can-go-long-way-bill-drayton-story.*

Ashoka United States. "Ashoka Envisions a World in Which Everyone is a Changemaker." Accessed Nov. 23, 2020. *https://www. ashoka.org/en-us/about-ashoka.*

Bornstein, David. "Changing the World on a Shoestring." *The Atlantic,* January 1998. *https://www.theatlantic.com/magazine/ archive/1998/01/changing-the-world-on-a-shoestring/377042/.*

Dictionary.com. "Multiplier Effect." Accessed Oct. 22, 2020. *https:// www.dictionary.com/browse/multiplier-effect.*

Entrepreneur Staff. "41 Percent of Gen Z-ers Plan to Become Entrepreneurs (Infographic)." *Entrepreneur,* Jan. 15, 2019. *https:// www.entrepreneur.com/article/326354.*

Forbes. "From Refugee to Venture Capitalist to Social Impact Pioneer | Forbes." Aug. 6, 2018. Video, 5:00. *https://www.youtube. com/watch?v=vSFqGovqyXk.*

Forbes. "The Social Impact Revolution is Here | Forbes." Jun. 25, 2018. Video, 2:32. *https://www.youtube.com/watch?v=WhVjcrR-Jpjo.*

Friedman, Milton. "A Friedman Doctrine—The Social Responsibility of Business Is to Increase Its Profits." *The New York Times,* Sept. 13, 1970. *https://www.nytimes.com/1970/09/13/ archives/a-friedman-doctrine-the-social-responsibility-of-business-is-to.html.*

Global Impact Investing Network. "Impact Investing." Accessed Jul. 13, 2020. *https://thegiin.org/impact-investing/.*

Global Policy Forum. "The Rise and Rise of NGOs." Accessed Aug. 24, 2020. *https://www.globalpolicy.org/component/content/ article/176/31937.html#:~:text=The%20first%20international%20 NGO%20was,for%20many%20organisations%20that%20followed.*

History.com. "Civil Rights Movement." Accessed Nov. 23, 2020. *https://www.history.com/topics/black-history/civil-rights-movement#:~:text=The%20civil%20rights%20movement%20was,law%20in%20the%20United%20States.*

How Do You Change the World? Become a Social Entrepreneur. Interview by Scott London. *Scott London.* March 2012. *http:// scott.london/interviews/drayton.html.*

Investopedia. "Corporate Social Responsibility (CSR)." Accessed Oct. 16, 2020. *https://www.investopedia.com/terms/c/corp-social-responsibility.asp.*

Mudaliar, Abhilash and Hannah Dithrich. *Sizing the Impact Investing Market.* New York: The GIIN, 2019.

Socialedge. "Muhammad Yunus—Grameen Bank." Feb. 5, 2008. Video, 6:59. *https://www.youtube.com/watch?v=TPk2gRuIdjo.*

Schwartz, Ariel. "What is Social Impact Anyways?." *The Center for Social Impact Strategy,* Aug. 30, 2017. *https://www.bnnbloomberg.ca/jeff-bezos-donating-10-billion-barely-dents-his-surging-fortune-1.1391945.*

Sir Ronald Cohen. "Bio." Accessed Aug. 10, 2020. *https://sirronaldcohen.org/bio.*

Social Entrepreneurs Don't Want to Help. They Want to Change the World. Interview by Parallel Worlds. *Parallel Worlds.* (n.d.) *https://www.egonzehnder.com/cdn/serve/article-pdf/1513691150-c700cbda2b13bb4b6440f602b8d23ef1.pdf.*

Summerfield, Richard. "The Impact of Social Entrepreneurship on Economic Growth." *Financier Worldwide Magazine,* May 2020. *https://www.financierworldwide.com/the-impact-of-social-entrepreneurship-on-economic-growth#.X5zyVC2z3Up.*

TEDx Talks. "A History of Microfinance | Muhammad Yunus | TEDxVienna." Jan. 18, 2012. Video, 23:47. *https://www.youtube.com/watch?v=6UCuWxWiMaQ*.

The Impact Revolution: Reshaping Capitalism. Interview by DLD Sync. *DLD Sync*. Oct. 5, 2020. *https://dldnews.com/sync/dld-sync-sir-ronald-cohen-impact-investing/*.

The Nobel Prize. "Muhammad Yunus—Biographical." Accessed Jul. 14, 2020. *https://www.nobelprize.org/prizes/peace/2006/yunus/biographical/*.

The Phrase Finder. "The Meaning and Origin of the Expression: Give a Man a Fish, and You Feed Him for a Day; Show Him How to Catch Fish, and You Feed Him for a Lifetime." Accessed Aug. 13, 2020. *https://www.phrases.org.uk/meanings/give-a-man-a-fish.html*.

Zhivago, Kristin. "Business Makes the World Go Round." *Kristin's Wisdom* (blog). Sept. 10, 2018. *https://kristinswisdom.com/business-makes-the-world-go-round/*.

CHAPTER 2: WHY NOW?

Association of Corporate Citizenship Professionals. "Corporate Social Responsibility: A Brief History." Accessed Aug. 4, 2020. *https://www.accprof.org/ACCP/ACCP/About_the_Field/Blogs/Blog_Pages/Corporate-Social-Responsibility-Brief-History.aspx*.

B Corporation. "How Did the B Corp Movement Start?" Accessed Aug. 6, 2020. *https://bcorporation.net/faq-item/how-did-b-corp-movement-start*.

Bowen, Howard R. *Social Responsibilities of the Businessman*. Iowa City: University of Iowa Press, 2013.

Carnegie, Andrew. *The Gospel of Wealth*. New York: Carnegie Corporation of New York, 2017.

Deloitte. "Driving Corporate Growth Through Social Impact: Four Corporate Archetypes to Maximize Your Social Impact." Accessed July 19, 2020. *https://www2.deloitte.com/us/en/pages/operations/articles/driving-corporate-growth-through-social-impact.html/*

Foundation of Change. s.v. "The World's First Permanent but Flexible 'Community Savings Account'." Accessed Aug. 2, 2020. *https://www.clevelandfoundation100.org/foundation-of-change/invention/goffs-vision/.*

Lego Braille Bricks. "Introducing Lego Braille Bricks." Accessed Aug. 6, 2020. *https://www.legobraillebricks.com.*

OneChild. "Our Vision and Mission." Accessed Dec. 20, 2020. *https://www.onechild.ca/our-vision-mission/.*

Operation Beautiful. "Operation Beautiful." Accessed Aug. 8, 2020.

Rapid Transition Alliance. "The Decline of the Single Bottom Line and the Growth of B-Corps." *Rapid Transition Alliance*, Aug. 16, 2019. *https://www.rapidtransition.org/stories/new-economics-the-rise-of-the-b-corp/.*

Saïd Business School. "Social-Impact Industry Support." Accessed Aug. 7, 2020. *https://www.sbs.ox.ac.uk/programmes/mbas/oxford-mba/career-development-centre/social-impact-industry-support.*

"Social Return on Investments." Accessed Dec. 20, 2020. *https://www.sopact.com/social-return-on-investments-sroi.*

The Center for Social Impact Strategy. "What is Social Impact Anyways?" *Social Impact Fundamentals*, Aug. 30, 2017. *https://csis.upenn.edu/news/what-is-social-impact-anyways/.*

The Journal of Student Science and Technology. "Online Research Coop Program." Accessed Dec. 18, 2020. *https://journal.fsst.ca/jsst/index.php/jsst/pages/view/coop.*

The Melvin and Bren Simon Foundation. "The Pay it Forward Movement." Accessed Aug. 8, 2020. *https://brensimon.com/the-pay-it-forward-movement/.*

CHAPTER 3: FROM HARDSHIPS TO INSPIRATION

Kim, Larry. "19 Short Inspirational Quotes for Overcoming Adversity." *Inc.com*, May 28, 2015. *https://www.inc.com/larry-kim/19-short-inspirational-quotes-for-overcoming-adversity.html.*

Malala Fund. "Malala's Story." Accessed Oct. 9, 2020. *https://malala.org/malalas-story.*

Tykocinski, Orit and Ortmann, Andreas. "The Lingering Effects of Our Past Experiences: The Sunk-Cost Fallacy and the Inaction-Inertia Effect." *Social and Personality Psychology Compass* 5, no. 9 (2011): 653-664.

CHAPTER 4: PURPOSE OVER PROFIT

Charitywater. "The Spring—The charity: water story." Feb. 13, 2020. Video, 19:42. *https://www.youtube.com/watch?v=bdBG5VO01e0.*

Frank, Robert. "Don't Envy the Super-Rich, They Are Miserable." *The Wall Street Journal*, March 9, 2011. *https://www.wsj.com/articles/BL-WHB-4703.*

INBOUND. "Scott Harrison | INBOUND 2018 Spotlight." Sept. 7, 2018. Video, 1:11:50. *https://www.youtube.com/watch?v=V4E1t2yIZlc.*

Karns, Christina. "Why a Grateful Brain is a Giving One." *Greater Good Magazine,* Dec. 19, 2017. *https://greatergood.berkeley.edu/ article/item/why_a_grateful_brain_is_a_giving_one.*

Smith, Jeremy Adam. "How to Find Your Purpose in Life." *Greater Good Magazine,* Jan. 10, 2018. *https://greatergood.berkeley.edu/ article/item/how_to_find_your_purpose_in_life.*

CHAPTER 5: COMMUNITY IMPACT

African Impact Initiative. "African Impact Rural Health Care Project (Shortened Version)." Jan 30, 2019. Video, 5:07. *https://www. youtube.com/watch?v=eljgsnQdTrE.*

African Impact Initiative. "Impacting Africa Through Our Youth." Accessed July 23, 2020. *https://www.africanimpact.ca.*

Florida National University Admin. "Why is Community Service Important?" *Florida National University News,* April 8, 2013. *https://www.fnu.edu/community-service-important/#:~:- text=Engaging%20in%20community%20service%20provides,- those%20who%20need%20it%20most.*

Hospital for Special Surgery. "Living with Chronic Pain." *Scleroderma, Vasculitis & Myositis eNewsletter,* Sept. 15, 2013. *https:// www.rapidtransition.org/stories/new-economics-the-rise-of-the- b-corp/.*

Random Acts of Kindness Foundation. "We Make a Living by What We Get. We Make a Life by What We Give." Accessed Jul. 25, 2020. *https://www.randomactsofkindness.org/kindness- quotes/282-we-make-a-living-by.*

"Trafficking in Persons in Canada, 2016." statcan.gc. Accessed July 23, 2020. *https://www150.statcan.gc.ca/n1/pub/85-005-x/2018001/ article/54979-eng.htm.*

CHAPTER 6: POWER OF KINDNESS

Aknin, Lara B, Christopher P. Barrington-Leigh, Elizabeth W. Dunn, John F. Helliwell, Robert Biswas-Diener, Imelda Kemeza, Paul Nyende, Claire Ashton-James, and Michael I. Norton. "Prosocial Spending and WellBeing: Cross-Cultural Evidence for a Psychological Universal." *American Psychological Association* 104, No. 4, 635-652. *https://www.apa.org/pubs/journals/releases/psp-104-4-635.pdf.*

Boraz, James and Alexander, Shoshana. "The Helper's High." *Greater Good Magazine*, Feb. 1, 2010. *https://greatergood.berkeley.edu/article/item/the_helpers_high.*

Cassity, Jessica. "Why One Act of Kindness is Usually Followed by Another." *Goodnet*, Dec. 24, 2014. *https://www.goodnet.org/articles/one-act-kindness-usually-followed-by-another?-source=post_page------------------------.*

Cohen, Sidney. "Small Acts of Kindness Have Big Impact in the N.W.T. Amid Pandemic." *CBC News*, April 23, 2020. *https://www.cbc.ca/news/canada/north/nwt-pandemic-acts-of-kindness-1.5542324.*

Hauch, Valerie. "Kindness Pays Off, Study Finds." *Toronto Star*, May 18, 2011. *https://www.thestar.com/life/health_wellness/diseases_cures/2011/05/18/kindness_pays_off_study_finds.html.*

Pressman, Sarah D, Tara L Kraft, and Marie P. Cross. "It's Good to Do Good and Receive Good: The Impact of a 'Pay It Forward' Style Kindness." *Journal of Positive Psychology* 10, no. 4 (2014): 1-10.

Lyubomirsky, Sonja, Kennon M Sheldon, and David Schkade. "Pursuing Happiness: The Architecture of Sustainable Change." *Review of General Psychology* 9, no. 2 (2005): 111-131.

Random Acts of Kindness. "Kindness Health Facts." Accessed Jul. 16, 2020. *https://www.dartmouth.edu/wellness/emotional/ rakhealthfacts.pdf.*

TEDx Talks. "The Power of Kindness | Orly Wahba | TEDxStPeterPort." April 1, 2016. Video, 21:31. *https://www.youtube.com/ watch?v=_DawgEK9muY.*

TEDx Talks. "Kindness is Your Superpower | Marly Q | TEDxJWUNorthMiami." Feb 28, 2018. Video, 20:39. *https://www. youtube.com/watch?v=guoFRPYD7aU.*

TEDx Talks. "Why Everyday Kindness and Simple Giving Matter | Jenny Schell | TEDxColoradoSprings." Jan. 5, 2017. Video, 10:35. *https://www.youtube.com/watch?v=FfwFUjVEIl4.*

Zaki, Jamil. "Kindness Contagion." *Scientific American*, July 26, 2016. *https://www.scientificamerican.com/article/kindness-contagion/.*

CHAPTER 7: EVERYDAY ADVOCACY

American Psychological Association. "Harmful Masculinity and Violence." *American Psychological Association*, Sept. 2018. *https://www.apa.org/pi/about/newsletter/2018/09/harmful-masculinity.*

Black Lives Matter. "About." Accessed Sept. 23, 2020. *https://blacklivesmatter.com/about/.*

Black Lives Matter. "Herstory." Accessed Sept. 23, 2020. *https:// blacklivesmatter.com/herstory/.*

Buchanan, Larry, Quoctryng Bui, and Jugal K. Patel. "Black Lives Matter May Be the Largest Movement in U.S. History." *The New York Times,* July 3, 2020. *https://www.nytimes.com/interactive/2020/07/03/us/george-floyd-protests-crowd-size.html.*

Canadian Women's Foundation. "About Us." Accessed Aug. 5, 2020. *https://canadianwomen.org/?gclid=CjoKCQiA34OBBh-CcARIsAG32uvNDdShG1aC1klXdA_SM6GXLeHB7PPR6WOK-dESNsO7mxAWocE7JWGpUaAmAuEALw_wcB.*

Ferré-Sadurní, Luis, and Jesse McKinley. "N.Y. Bans Chokeholds and Approves Other Measures to Restrict Police." *The New York Times,* June 17, 2020. *https://www.nytimes.com/2020/06/12/nyregion/50a-repeal-police-floyd.html.*

Goodreads. "Malala Yousafzai Quotes." Accessed Aug. 27, 2020. *https://www.goodreads.com/quotes/930638-when-the-whole-world-is-silent-even-one-voice-becomes.*

Hill, Evan, Ainara Tiefenthäler, Christiaan Triebert, Drew Jordan, Haley Willis, and Robin Stein. "How George Floyd was Killed in Police Custody." *The New York Times,* May 31, 2020. *https://www.nytimes.com/2020/05/31/us/george-floyd-investi-gation.html.*

Merriam-Webster. s.v. "Advocacy." Accessed Sept. 5, 2020. *https://www.merriam-webster.com/dictionary/advocacy.*

Next Gen Men. "About Us." Accessed Aug. 5, 2020. *https://www.nextgenmen.ca/.*

Sentinel, Orlando. "Florida Teen Trayvon Martin is Shot and Killed." *History,* Feb. 26, 2012. *https://www.history.com/this-day-in-history/florida-teen-trayvon-martin-is-shot-and-killed.*

The Phrase Finder. "Rome Wasn't Built in a Day." Accessed Sept. 5, 2020. *https://www.phrases.org.uk/meanings/rome-wasnt-built-in-a-day.html.*

White Ribbon. "About White Ribbon." Accessed Aug. 5, 2020. *https://www.whiteribbon.ca/.*

CHAPTER 8: PURPOSE IN CORPORATE & THE IMPACT OF BUSINESS

Ann Mei Chang. "Biography." Accessed July 13, 2020. *https://www.annmei.com/bio.*

Ben & Jerry's. "Our History." Accessed Aug. 15, 2020. *https://www.benandjerrys.ca/en/about-us#5timeline.*

Exeleon. "Melody Hossaini: Transforming Lives by Harvesting Human Potentials." *Exeleon Magazine,* (n.d.). *https://exeleon-magazine.com/melody-hossaini-transforming-lives/*

Fulphil. "Home." Accessed Aug. 26, 2020. *https://fulphil.org/.*

GSDRC. "Executive Summary." Accessed July 13, 2020. *https://gsdrc.org/topic-guides/the-social-impact-of-private-sector-development/executive-summary/*

"Harvard Business School. "Michael E. Porter." Accessed Aug. 28, 2020. *https://www.hbs.edu/faculty/Pages/profile.aspx?-facId=6532&view=awards.*

Lego Braille Bricks. "About Lego Braille Bricks." Accessed Aug. 27, 2020. *https://www.legobraillebricks.com/about.*

Lego Braille Bricks. "Learning Through Play." Accessed Aug. 14, 2020. *https://www.legobraillebricks.com/learningthroughplay.*

Lego. "Ellen MacArthur Foundation and LEGO Group Join Forces to Accelerate the Move Towards a Circular Economy." *Lego,* Aug. 30, 2020. *https://www.lego.com/en-in/aboutus/news/2020/august/ellen-macarthur-foundation/.*

Melody Hossaini. "Advancement of Young People & Women in Social Enterprise." Oct. 19, 2015. Video, 3:07. *https://www.youtube.com/watch?v=A-lGtNom22E.*

Nemeth, Alexandra. "Quotes from Social Entrepreneurs to Inspire You to Change the World." *Social Enterprise* (blog), *Moving-Worlds*, Nov. 25, 2019. *https://blog.movingworlds.org/quotes-from-social-entrepreneurs-to-inspire-you-to-change-the-world/.*

Talks at Google. "Radical Innovation for Greater Social Good | Ann Mei Chang | Talks at Google." Feb. 19, 2019. Video, 55:01. *https://www.youtube.com/watch?v=rRIsuCMa85Y.*

TED. "Michael Porter: Why Business Can Be Good at Solving Social Problems." Oct. 7, 2013. Video, 16:28. *https://www.youtube.com/watch?v=oiIh5YYDR20.*

TEDx Talks. "Ending Global Poverty: Let's Think Like Silicon Valley | Ann Mei Chang | TEDxMidAtlantic." Jan. 10, 2017. Video, 12:24. *https://www.youtube.com/watch?v=cgUho7hiZ34.*

TEDx Talks. "The Social Enterprise Revolution: Melody Hossaini at TEDxKLWomen 2013." Mar. 24, 2014. Video, 17:49. *https://www.youtube.com/watch?v=95f8RV_YdKY.*

Tiffany Yau. "My Story." Accessed Aug. 14, 2020. *https://www.tiffanyyau.info/my-story.*

Tran, Khai. "Bringing Entrepreneurship Education to Students in Underserved Communities: Interview with Tiffany Yau." *Forbes,* Jan. 16, 2020. *https://www.forbes.com/sites/khaitran/2020/01/16/bringing-entrepreneurship-education-to-students-in-underserved-communities-interview-with-tiffany-yau/?sh=-234fa5244a69.*

Upswell. "Upswell 2018 (Ann Mei Chang)." Jan 17, 2019. Video, 19:36. *https://www.youtube.com/watch?v=dO1IZLonfTk&feature=emb_logo.*

Valet, Vicky. "The World's Most Reputable Companies for Corporate Responsibility 2019." *Forbes,* Sept. 17, 2019. *https://www.*

forbes.com/sites/vickyvalet/2019/09/17/the-worlds-most-repu-table-companies-for-corporate-responsibility-2019/?sh=3e-57c4a679bd.

CHAPTER 9: YOUNG IMPACT

Bags of Books. "About." Accessed Jul. 15, 2020. *https://www.bag-sofbooks.org/about.*

Jason Feifer. Interview by Eric Koester. *Creator Series.* Oct. 5, 2020. *https://www.dropbox.com/s/qj196tj3zjp4grr/Jason%20Feifer%20 -%20Creator%20Series%20-%2010-5-2020.mp4?dl=0.*

KIPP. "About." Accessed Jul. 15, 2020. *https://www.kipp. org/?gclid=CjoKCQiAx9mABhDoARIsAEfpavS8wQKb-pnf53eG-D8jVmMMqtDcfRHegL-NQfu-nLtnpBozdT-qA-sYYaAmr3EALw_wcB.*

TEDx Talks. "Wired for Innovation | Ilona Dougherty | TEDxUW." May 11, 2017. Video, 17:59. *https://www.youtube.com/watch?v=-mobQ-r6k5xY.*

University of Waterloo. "Ilona Dougherty." Accessed Jul. 13, 2020. *https://uwaterloo.ca/school-environment-enterprise-develop-ment/people-profiles/ilona-dougherty.*

University of Waterloo. "Youth & Innovation Project." Accessed Jul. 13, 2020. *https://uwaterloo.ca/youth-and-innovation/.*

CHAPTER 10: TAKING A LEAP OF FAITH

Arnold-Smeets, Leah. "4 Social Entrepreneurs Who Changed Careers and Changed the World." *PayScale Career News*, Jul. 29, 2016. *https://www.payscale.com/career-news/2016/07/change-careers-change-world.*

Hall, Alan. "Are You an Entrepreneur? The Leap of Faith." *Forbes,* Jun. 4, 2012. *https://www.forbes.com/sites/alanhall/2012/06/04/ are-you-an-entrpreneur-the-leap-of-faith/?sh=df3102e3da0a.*

Moore, *Mark H. Creating Public Value: Strategic Management in Government.* Cambridge: Harvard University Press, 1997.

The Phrase Finder. "Leap of Faith." Accessed Jul. 10, 2020. *https:// www.phrases.org.uk/bulletin_board/28/messages/1051.html.*

CHAPTER 11: CHALLENGING THE CONVENTIONAL

Flores, Glenn, Milagros Abreu, Ilan Schwartz and Maria Hill. "The Importance of Language and Culture in Pediatric Care: Case Studies from the Latino Community." *The Journal of Pediatrics* 137, no. 6 (2013): 842-848. *https://www.researchgate.net/ profile/Glenn_Flores/publication/.*

Gauthier, JF, Marc Penzel and Arnobio Morelix. "This is What COVID-19 Did to Start-ups in China." *World Economic Forum,* May 7, 2020. *https://www.weforum.org/agenda/2020/05/ covid-19-s-coronavirus-startups-china-funding/?fbclid=I- wARoZ1rYTXB8Ljg6dLHhZqzhk6noGmoLqa95Drg- 3migp-w7Cp84AfeCS4brA.*

Injury Facts. "Hot Car Deaths." Accessed Oct. 22, 2020. *https:// injuryfacts.nsc.org/motor-vehicle/motor-vehicle-safety-issues/ hotcars/.*

Safian, Robert. "Why Apple is the World's Most Innovative Company." *Fast Company,* Feb. 21, 2018. *https://www.fastcompany. com/40525409/why-apple-is-the-worlds-most-innovative-company.*

Welch, Denice E and Lawrence S. Welch. "The Importance of Language in International Knowledge Transfer." *Manage-*

ment International Review 48, no. 3 (2008): 339-360. *https:// www.researchgate.net/profile/Lawrence_Welch/publication/.*

Workspace Digital. "30 Of Our Favorite Quotes on Innovation." Accessed Oct. 8, 2020. *http://workspace.digital/30-favorite-quotes-innovation/.*

CHAPTER 12: PUTTING IT ALL TOGETHER: THE MAGICAL MOVEMENT OF IMPACT

Dean Hankey. "The Pay it Forward and Profit Guy!" Accessed July 10, 2020. *http://www.deanhankey.com/.*

Made in the USA
Columbia, SC
25 May 2021